TASTY. HEALTHY. CHEAP.

TO MOM, DAD, AND MY BROTHER,
DAVID, WHO SUPPORTED ME
WHEN I DROPPED OUT OF UNI
TO MAKE INTERNET VIDEOS.
LOOK, I HAVE A BOOK NOW!

Inspiring | Educating | Creating | Entertaining

Brimming with creative inspiration, how-to projects, and useful information to enrich your everyday life, quarto.com is a favorite destination for those pursuing their interests and passions.

© 2023 Quarto Publishing Group USA Inc.
Text and Photography © 2023 Kevin Tatar

First Published in 2023 by The Harvard Common Press, an imprint of The Quarto Group, 100 Cummings Center, Suite 265-D, Beverly, MA 01915, USA.
T (978) 282-9590 F (978) 283-2742
Quarto.com

The Harvard Common Press titles are also available at discount for retail, wholesale, promotional, and bulk purchase. For details, contact the Special Sales Manager by email at specialsales@quarto.com or by mail at The Quarto Group, Attn: Special Sales Manager, 100 Cummings Center, Suite 265-D, Beverly, MA 01915, USA.

27 26 25 24 23   1 2 3 4 5

ISBN: 978-0-7603-8220-2

Digital edition published in 2023
eISBN: 978-0-7603-8221-9

Library of Congress Cataloging-in-Publication Data

Tatar, Kevin, author.
Tasty, healthy, cheap : budget-friendly recipes with exciting flavors / Kevin Tatar.
  LCCN 2022049439 (print) | LCCN 2022049440 (ebook) |
ISBN
  9780760382202 (paperback) | ISBN 9780760382219 (ebook)
1. Quick and easy cooking. 2. Cookbooks
LCC TX833.5 .T384 2023 (print) | LCC TX833.5 (ebook) |
  DDC 641.5/12--dc23/eng/20221114

Design and layout: Burge Agency
Cover Image: Kevin Tatar
Photography: Kevin Tatar

Printed in China

TASTY. HEALTHY. CHEAP.

BUDGET-FRIENDLY RECIPES WITH EXCITING FLAVORS

KEVIN TATAR
CREATOR OF KWOOWK

HARVARD COMMON PRESS

CONTENTS

Introduction 06

CHAPTER 1:
BASICS 10
Equipment 12

My Staple Ingredients 14

Basic Techniques and
Terminology 18

Basic Recipes 22

CHAPTER 2:
BREAKFAST TIME 30
Foolproof Breakfasts 32

Global Breakfasts 44

Egg-cellent Breakfasts 48

CHAPTER 3:
ON THE GO OR AT THE DESK 54
Handheld Meals 56

Salads 67

CHAPTER 4:
INSTANT CLASSICS 78
Meals That Got Me
Through College 80

Comfort Foods 90

CHAPTER 5:
DINNERTIME 98
Dinner for One 100
Date Night Recipes 108

CHAPTER 6:
PASTA AND BOWL FOOD 118
Pasta 120
Bowl Food 128

CHAPTER 7:
PARTY ESSENTIALS 138
Crowd Pleasers 140
Finger Foods 148

CHAPTER 8:
SWEETS AND TREATS 156
Desserts 158
Sweet Tooth Snacks 167

Acknowledgments 172
About the Author 173
Index 174

INTRODUCTION

Welcome to my first book! You probably know me best as the creator behind the KWOOWK videos. Whether you've already tried some of my recipes by following along online or not, I am glad you decided to give this book a chance.

WHAT TO EXPECT IN THIS BOOK

This is not a fancy book! I developed these recipes so anyone, regardless of cooking experience, can make something delicious with easy-to-find ingredients and a minimal investment in cooking equipment. All recipes are easy to master and can (and likely will) become part of your weekly meal rotation.

In short, this book is all about getting you to make that first step in the kitchen confidently and own your failures while there!—or take the next step and cook more than you do today. I want you to discover the joy of combining everyday ingredients into new dishes that *you* can modify as you see fit and that taste good, too. And, yes, some of your attempts at these recipes may not come out exactly as you planned, at first, but you'll find it doesn't really matter: You will *always* end up with something to eat (okay, unless you truly walk away from the stove or oven!), and you should be proud of what you create.

THE RECIPES: IT ALL STARTED WITH TASTY AND CHEAP

While healthy (or healthy-ish) recipes are a big part of what I do (more on that in a bit!), I think most people started following me because they wanted tasty recipes they could make with minimal investment. I have a lot of fans still in college, or just getting out of school, and they mostly want fast, fresh meals that don't break the bank.

My biggest inspiration in my cooking journey was my grandma. When I was a kid, we cooked together for the whole family, and I was (at least in my mind) an essential part of this process. She made me understand the value of food as something that brings people together, something that's more than just fuel for your day. This is the spark that ignited my love for cooking.

A few years down the road, I left my home country of Romania to travel to the Netherlands for my studies. I was a clueless 18-year-old trying to figure out life, and cooking for myself was a priority. There was this stereotype that college cooking was BAD—instant noodles, frozen pizza, fast-food burgers, and the occasional deep-fried "kroketten" (a Dutch mystery meat formed into a log). Although I think these foods have their place, I didn't buy this idea. I started looking into ways I could, on a limited budget, make nutritious meals that I actually looked forward to eating.

I didn't do this to prove a point. I simply enjoyed it, and I wanted to share this joy with the world. I believe home cooking, especially for young people, is an essential skill that is part of a more sustainable

future. I took this idea, combined it with simple recipes approached from a curious and easy-to-understand perspective, and created the videos that you may know me from.

This book is a reflection of how I entered the vast world of cooking, as someone who knew next to nothing to start. You may notice I'm imprecise and informal in the way I write these things: I am not a formally trained chef; I am simply a guy who likes making food at home and sharing it with the world. But I do think there's value from this perspective, and I tried to give you as much value as I can in this book.

SO, WHAT IS HEALTHY?

"Healthy" is a big word that is also part of the title of the book you're reading right now. (Hi, again! Thanks for reading this!)

Most people don't know this, but I started cooking because of fitness-related goals. Yet, it didn't take long before I developed a distaste for the "food is just fuel" mentality that is all too common these days. I instead came to the realization that maybe a dish shouldn't just be a collection of numbers that determines how "healthy" I am.

Sure, healthy can mean nutritious, low in calories, low in sugar, high in fiber, or rich in probiotics. All these things are important, and they are often a consideration for the recipes I create. But I want you to understand that healthy can mean lots of things, and different things to different people. Whether you're eating a cookie because it reminds you of being a kid, savoring a piece of cake with friends for a special occasion, or devouring a plate of cheesy nachos by yourself after a tough week, there is no need to feel guilty. All these things fall under my definition of healthy! After all, in moderation, even "junk food" or sweets can be fuel—in this case, fuel for the mind or for social enjoyment!

Our relationship with food is complicated. I believe we shouldn't be so quick to slap labels on things. Just be mindful about what you're eating and be nice to yourself. The last thing I want you to do is to think of these recipes solely in terms of numbers. Flavor and satisfaction are important, too. So, whenever I use the word "healthy," I generally mean within a commonsense approach to eating, including lower in calories, nutritionally balanced, more veggies, less fat, less processed sugar, realistic portion sizes, etc. Take this word with a "grain of salt," and consider what healthy means to you. Now, go have some fun.

ADAPTING THE RECIPES

These recipes aren't exact blueprints you need to follow precisely. Many utilize techniques you can apply in your own ways, according to your preferences and needs.

Want to incorporate your favorite local and seasonal ingredients in a recipe? Go for it! After you've cooked a few recipes, maybe you'll combine two techniques from two different recipes in something new you dreamed up. There's a lot of room for creativity and experimentation in cooking, and nothing would make me happier than seeing you use these recipes as a springboard for your own creative cooking.

OWNING YOUR RESULTS

Of course, as you get more confident and creative in the kitchen, you might take more risks or pay less attention to your task at hand. So, when something goes wrong (because it will), don't get discouraged; look at it as an opportunity to improve. Look back at your process analytically, considering what effects every step had on the final product and where things might have gone awry: You'll be a better cook in no time with this approach.

However, please don't bring out your notebooks and treat this like math class or a precise science. That is unrealistic and unsustainable—just try to develop a feel for it over time, and acknowledge your mistakes in a nonjudgmental fashion. The kitchen is not a sacred place for precision and limitation. It should be a liberating environment where you're free to make creative decisions based on your imagination and your feelings.

In fact, something that always makes me happy is that, every time I mess up a recipe, I almost always think to myself while eating it, *You know, this is actually pretty tasty*!

COOKING INTUITIVELY

When you read these recipes and try to make them, focus on your feelings and intuitions, and use all of your senses in the process. This is a valuable skill for any cook to develop! Approach cooking from this book with a learning and self-developing mind-set: Don't just follow along blindly; teach yourself how to connect with the food you're cooking. I know it may sound abstract, but once you develop that connection, you'll understand your food on a different level.

For example, knowing when food is done is tied to observing it for doneness cues. Look and smell the onions in the pan. What color do they have? See how they behave when you move them. Taste and touch. Are they soft? Can you hear the sizzle in the pan? Do they look or smell like they're burning? Maybe it's time to turn the heat a bit lower even though I wrote instructions that say to cook it on high heat for another minute.

Listen to your intuition and trust your senses! You got this!
—Kevin Tatar

CHAPTER 1:
BASICS

Equipment   12

My Staple Ingredients   14

Basic Techniques and
Terminology   18

Basic Recipes   21

Boiled Eggs, the Easy Way   22

Veggie Stock from Scraps   23

Pickled Red Onions and
Other Things   24

Straightforward Chicken
Breast   25

Herby Yogurt Sauce
and Dip   26

Perfect Rice Every Time   27

EQUIPMENT

Let's get you set up and ready to cook with some essential concepts that will guide you through this book.

I'd say 99 percent of these recipes require basic, minimal kitchen equipment and tools. Even if you don't have all these things, don't worry; you can probably still create the recipes successfully with whatever you have on hand (unless you just moved into your own place and haven't bought a single pan yet!).

BAKING DISHES
If you are one of the lucky people who has an oven, take full advantage of it. A baking sheet is essential for your everyday oven needs. Use it to roast vegetables and proteins, bake cookies, and many other things. I also use a 9 × 13-inch (23 × 33 cm) glass baking dish for casseroles, lasagna, or mac and cheese.

CUTTING BOARD
Forget that tiny plastic cutting board that seems to come with every apartment. When it comes to cutting boards, my motto is the bigger the better. I have a large wooden board that's always on my counter for easy chopping and assembling. It's also advisable to have one cutting board for raw meats and another for things such as vegetables, nuts, etc., to avoid cross-contamination.

FOOD PROCESSOR OR BLENDER
I know these are different tools and technically used for different reasons, but I manage just fine with only one of them. Either tool will help with sauces, smoothies, soups, chopping, and many other things. Get heatproof versions for maximum versatility.

GARLIC PRESS
Although this might seem as if it's a totally unnecessary gadget, I use fresh garlic so much that I literally could not *not* use this. It's inconvenient to chop a tiny garlic clove and dirty a cutting board and a knife. This is better, trust me.

KNIVES
A good chef's knife is very important to have. It's a tool you will use for almost everything in this book!

RICE COOKER

This is not a necessity BUT, hear me out. If you eat a lot of rice, it's a lifesaver. My rice cooker cost $20 and does the job. It's super convenient to just turn it on and forget about it, and it makes perfect rice every single time.

SPATULAS, WOODEN SPOONS, AND SPIDERS

When it comes to stirring, frying, flipping, boiling, and overall manipulating of food that is actively cooking, I suggest keeping the following on hand: a rubber or silicone spatula, a sturdy wooden spoon, a wide plastic or metal spatula, and a spider for flipping things such as eggs, pancakes, or burgers, or removing items from water or hot oil.

Pro tip: Since it often lives in the same drawer, a whisk is indispensable for situations where you have to whisk things. (Hence the name!)

STORAGE CONTAINERS

My advice here is to buy a set of quality food storage containers that have tight-fitting lids as soon as you're able to. They'll be useful to either refrigerate or freeze leftovers and large quantities of food for later use and to avoid food waste. Also, make sure to get some glass jars with lids. Not only can you store pantry items such as flour and oats in them, but also homemade sauces and pickled stuff, and you can even freeze soups and other items in them if batch cooking for future meals.

Invest in a good chef's knife, even if it costs more than you'd like to spend. You don't need to go crazy though; just find one that is sharp, with a handle that is comfortable for you.

Why invest here? Well, this single knife can do just about any kitchen prep job you need to do. Though, if you have the budget, I also recommend a serrated knife for bread and soft vegetables such as tomatoes as well as a simple paring knife for more precise tasks.

PANS, SKILLETS, AND POTS

To cook, you will need something to cook in. To me, pans and skillets are kinda interchangeable: I have a few different sizes of nonstick pans, a large stainless-steel skillet for browning protein and veggies, and a saucepan.

I also suggest buying a large, deep soup pot with a lid for making soups and stocks, as well as a Dutch oven or other heavy-bottomed pot for braising, slow cooking, and a whole lot more.

MY STAPLE INGREDIENTS

Everyday cooking becomes easier when you can rely on a few essential ingredients kept handy in your pantry or fridge. These are my favorites, and the ones you'll see throughout the book. That said, once you start cooking, your staples may be a little different.

ACIDS

Acidity is a key element in balancing the flavor of a dish. Fresh lemon and lime juice are my favorites for this purpose, but stock up on vinegars as well. Rice vinegar is popular in my house, but apple cider vinegar and distilled white vinegar are equally effective at adding that splash to liven up the flavors.

CANNED BEANS

My love for canned beans has already become a bit of a meme in my community. I use chickpeas and black beans in lots of my recipes because they're just so versatile, inexpensive, tasty, and nutritious. Check out my Chickpea Wrap (page 60) and The Best Black Bean Burger You'll Ever Eat (page 100). Highly recommended!

CHICKEN

Chicken is, perhaps, my second most-used protein (behind beans, of course), for many reasons: (1) I'm just used to it; (2) It's inexpensive and convenient where I live; (3) I really like it. You'll probably notice this bias, so I just wanted to give you a head's-up.

EGGS

A staple if ever there was one. They're cheap, nutritious, and convenient. Eggs are used in many recipes in this book—you should definitely have them in your fridge.

FATS

Most of my cooking is done with a medium-priced extra-virgin olive oil. You don't need to buy top-of-the-line olive oil for your day-to-day cooking, but make sure to invest a little bit more in an oil you would use for salad dressings and sauces, and to drizzle over a finished dish to add a bit of extra fat, flavor, and silky mouthfeel. When a recipe calls for a neutral-flavored oil, my favorites are sunflower oil and peanut oil, but you can use any sort of vegetable oil with a higher smoke point, meaning it will perform well over a higher heat without reaching the smoking and burning point as soon as some other oils, such as olive oil.

When I do use butter, I always use unsalted butter to help manage the overall sodium in my foods. My recipes do not specify unsalted butter, so use what you have and prefer.

FRESH VEGETABLES

Take advantage of what's in season and local at your farmers' market or grocery store for less expensive, better-tasting veggies. Quality fresh vegetables will instantly upgrade your food, trust me. I like all vegetables, but my most common staples are bell peppers, carrots, broccoli, eggplant, potatoes, and tomatoes.

GARLIC, ONION, AND OTHER AROMATICS

Although part of the fresh vegetable category, I call out these ingredients separately as you will never catch me out of garlic, onions, fresh hot chiles, and fresh ginger. These ingredients have tons of flavor and form the base layer for many dishes. You can use them in almost anything: curry, guacamole, pasta sauces, salsa, soups, stir-fries, and so many more.

GOUDA CHEESE

I mention this because my use of Gouda might be a bit strange for my non-European readers. I use Gouda cheese A LOT because I'm based in the Netherlands (aka where Gouda comes from), and it's incredibly accessible and cheap here because it's locally produced. If you can't find Gouda or prefer something else, try cheddar, Gruyère, or pepper Jack in any recipe that calls for Gouda.

OATS

I always have old-fashioned rolled oats in my pantry. Not only can you create an unlimited array of cheap and nutritious breakfast dishes and desserts with them (like Peanut Butter Banana Baked Oats, page 35, or Cinnamon Apple Crumble, page 162), but they can also be used in other ways as a fiber-rich substitute for all-purpose flour, as in my Healthier Chocolate Lava Cake (page 158).

RICE

I use rice a lot as a base carb in my recipes, and you can use leftovers to make the most delicious fried rice. (Try The Leftover Fried Rice, page 80, to see what I mean.)

The type of rice you choose depends on your preference. I choose a short-grain sushi rice for the most part because I find that it provides the most versatility in my cooking. Other popular options that I use a lot include basmati, brown, and jasmine rice.

SWEETENERS AND SEASONINGS

HONEY AND MAPLE SYRUP
I do realize these are just liquid forms of sugar, but I virtually always choose to sweeten my dishes with them instead of refined granulated sugar. I find that honey and maple syrup also provide a deep, earthy flavor to recipes, and having them in liquid form makes them more versatile.

SOY SAUCE
I admit, I am a total soy boy. I never run out of soy sauce in my home. I have multiple bottles of different soy varieties and I use them all. Invest in a big bottle of quality soy sauce and refrigerate it for maximum taste. You can use it in cooking, in marinades, in dressings and sauces, and as a general umami finisher for your meals.

SPICES AND HERBS (DRIED AND FRESH)
The easiest way to improve the flavor of any dish is with herbs and spices! I suggest finding your favorites and always having them on hand to flavor-blast any meal. My essentials include black pepper, smoked paprika, garlic powder, dried thyme, ground cinnamon, and, of course, salt. Speaking of salt, I use kosher salt for just about everything when it comes to cooking. Its bigger, flaky grain makes it easier to control the amount of salt I'm adding using my hands. I also use flaky sea salt for finishing purposes, such as topping chocolate brownies for a salty, crunchy contrast.

As for fresh herbs, they obviously don't have the shelf life of dried, but add irresistible pops of flavor to your cooking, especially when added just before serving. Pastas, sauces, marinades, and really anything, even nachos, can be a candidate for using fresh herbs for flavor, and you can use the leftovers for stocks so you don't waste anything. My go-tos are fresh parsley, chives, cilantro, and basil.

TORTILLAS
These wraps are essential in my kitchen. They are a delicious delivery mechanism for a quick, satisfying meal when you're in a hurry, and they can also be used many ways.

Because I haven't honed my from-scratch tortilla-making skills, I buy these in the grocery store for convenience. I always have small 6-inch (15 cm) tortillas on hand for any taco-related recipes, and I use large 12-inch (30 cm) tortillas for wraps and burritos.

YOGURT
Full-fat plain Greek yogurt is my go-to base for healthier sauces and dips, nutritious desserts, and breakfast dishes. You can even marinate meat and poultry in this stuff: It's simply an overpowered and underutilized ingredient you must have.

BASIC TECHNIQUES AND TERMINOLOGY

There are a few basic techniques and terms I want to go over because I use them a lot and you need to know how to do them to create the recipes in this book. Don't worry—everything's simple and always gets easier with practice.

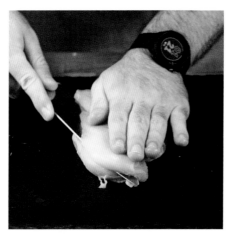

BUTTERFLYING
To cook thicker or unevenly sized pieces of protein, such as a chicken breast or pork chop, evenly and easily, we sometimes do something called "butterflying" it. This just means to cut through the middle of the protein horizontally, using a sawing motion, but without cutting all the way through, so you can open it like a book, creating a thinner cut of meat.

COOKING UNTIL FRAGRANT
When cooking aromatics—chiles, garlic, onions, and spices—a good cue to look for (or, rather, *smell*) is that pleasant scent that releases into the air that will alert anyone in the house that food is on the way. When that happens, whatever aromatics are in your pan are ready for the next step of the cooking process.

CUTTING AGAINST THE GRAIN

The "grain" refers to the direction of the muscle fibers in meat. To cut against them means to cut in a perpendicular direction to them, across the fibers, shortening them, which makes the final cooked pieces more tender to eat.

DEGLAZING THE PAN

The act of deglazing a pan refers to stirring some liquid into a hot pan after cooking a piece of meat or vegetables to help release the browned, caramelized bits (see Fond, page 21) stuck to the bottom of the pan. Those bits have lots of delicious flavors you want incorporated into your dish or sauce.

FINELY/ROUGHLY CHOPPED

When chopping anything it's important to go for a specific size, depending on its purpose, and to chop ingredients uniformly in size so they cook at the same rate. For example, I like using finely chopped herbs in dips and sauces and for garnish, but I will go for a less careful rough chop (kinda randomly chopping in bigger pieces) for soups and such, and a smaller in-between dice for dishes that are quicker cooking.

FOLDING A BURRITO

Mastering this technique will automatically make you cooler, and I don't think I have to explain why. Practice a couple of times and you'll be a burrito-folding master in no time.

Lay a tortilla on a flat work surface.

Place your burrito fillings just below the midline of the tortilla, leaving some space on the sides.

Fold in the sides until they reach the filling, and while holding them down, use your thumbs to pull the bottom of the tortilla up and over the filling.

Tuck in the leftover sides under the main fold and finish by rolling the burrito tightly.

FOND

The fond is the browned, caramelized bits of food that remain in the pan after cooking meat or vegetables. It's full of flavor and should never be discarded.

REDUCING

Simmering liquid until some of the water or other liquid evaporates, creating a thicker, more concentrated consistency and flavor.

SALTING PASTA WATER

A lot of chefs and random internet cooking experts will suggest salting your pasta water until it "tastes like the ocean." And look, I don't wanna pretend to know more than they do, but that direction is unnecessarily vague and could lead to adding way too much salt. A simple rule I follow is for every 1 pound (454 g) of pasta being cooked, add 1 tablespoon (10 g) of kosher salt. Use more or less, depending on how salty your other ingredients are.

SAUTÉING

To cook food quickly in a pan over a higher heat with a small amount of oil while tossing and stirring.

STIR-FRYING

A variation of sauté, but a bit quicker and more intense. This is my go-to cooking technique, and it refers to cooking ingredients quickly over high heat in hot oil, tossing and stirring vigorously.

BOILED EGGS, THE EASY WAY

YIELD: MAKES 4 EGGS

The humble boiled egg. It's not as flashy as its fancy and exciting egg friends, such as poached eggs and French omelets, but it's always there for you when you need it. Boiled eggs are simple, practical, delicious, and versatile. This is an easy guide to making any sort of boiled egg—from soft to hard.

INSTRUCTIONS

Fill a large pot with enough water to completely submerge the eggs and bring it to a boil over high heat. Once boiling, immediately turn the heat to medium-low and keep the water at a gentle boil.

Using a spider or a large spoon, carefully lower the eggs into the water. Cook for 7 to 12 minutes, depending on how soft or hard you want them boiled (7 minutes = soft-boiled; 8 minutes = medium soft-boiled [my favorite]; 9 minutes = medium-boiled; 12 minutes = hard-boiled).

While the eggs cook, fill a large bowl with ice and water.

When the eggs have cooked to your liking, immediately transfer them to the ice bath and let cool for 2 to 3 minutes. This will stop the cooking process and make them easier to peel.

Pro tip: *Peel the eggs under a stream of cold water to remove the shell easily.*

INGREDIENTS

4 large eggs

VEGGIE STOCK FROM SCRAPS

YIELD: MAKES ABOUT 3 QUARTS (2.8 L)

I have to admit, I usually have a hard time making things from scratch, just because it's not as convenient, but in this case, the amazing flavor of this stock cannot be overstated. Collect the vegetable scraps, skins, and leftovers that you use throughout the week in a zip-top bag and throw it in the freezer until you're ready to cook. Keep things like potato skins and bits, carrot peels and trimmings, fresh herb stalks and unused herbs, corn cobs, asparagus trimmings, chopped broccoli stalks, onion skins and leftovers, but stay away from strongly flavored vegetables, such as Brussels sprouts and turnips, that can take over the flavor of your stock. When the bag is full, create the best stock from what would otherwise be trash. You can use it for soups, sauces, braised meat dishes, and anything else needing a flavorful liquid. Isn't that cool? Come on, admit that it's cool.

INGREDIENTS

1 large zip-top bag full of veggie scraps

1 onion, halved

1 head garlic, halved horizontally to expose the cloves

1 celery stalk, chopped

1 small bunch fresh thyme (optional)

Kosher salt

INSTRUCTIONS

Empty your scrap bag into a large soup pot and add the onion, garlic, celery, and thyme (if using). Add enough water to fully submerge the veggies and bring to a boil over medium-high heat. Once boiling, turn the heat to low and simmer the stock, partially covered with a lid, for about 30 minutes. Taste and season with salt.

Strain the broth through a fine-mesh sieve and discard the solids. Use immediately, or refrigerate in an airtight container for up to 5 days, or freeze for up to 4 months.

PICKLED RED ONIONS (AND OTHER THINGS)

YIELD: MAKES 1 QUART (960 ML) PICKLES

I used to think pickling was a complex and highly precise process that I could never implement in my cooking. That is until I figured out that, well, it's actually extremely easy. The first thing I learned how to pickle was red onion, and this has become essential in my day-to-day cooking. Here's a really low-effort way to make your own pickles and have them for a long time in the fridge.

INSTRUCTIONS

To start your pickle: Decide what you want to pickle (for example, let's say red onion), prep it (thinly slice, in this case), and fill a 1-quart (960 ml) glass mason jar with a lid with the ingredient. Make sure everything is loosely packed and doesn't fill the jar entirely.

To create added flavor: Add flavor enhancers to the jar to taste (if using). I add 2 or 3 garlic cloves and a couple of thyme sprigs, but use the flavors you like.

To make the brine: In a small saucepan over high heat, combine the vinegar, water, and a generous sprinkle of salt. Bring to a boil. Once boiling, turn off the heat, then pour the liquid into the jar, completely covering the red onion (or whatever you're pickling). Let cool to room temperature, uncovered, then close the jar with a tight-fitting lid and transfer to your fridge. You can keep these pickles for several months, but I suspect they will be gone before that.

INGREDIENTS FOR THINGS TO PICKLE:

Thinly sliced red onion

Carrot sticks (small to medium-size)

Green beans, trimmed

Sliced fresh red chiles

Sliced cucumbers

INGREDIENTS FOR OPTIONAL FLAVOR ADDITIONS:

Fresh herbs (such as thyme or rosemary)

Garlic cloves, peeled

Black peppercorns

Mustard seeds

Red pepper flakes

STRAIGHTFORWARD CHICKEN BREAST

YIELD: MAKES 2 BREASTS

Chicken breast gets a bad rep for blandness and dryness, but that's mostly because many people have no idea how to cook it properly. This is juicy, flavorful chicken breast that you can whip up in less than 10 minutes.

INGREDIENTS

2 boneless, skinless chicken breasts

Kosher salt and ground black pepper

Vegetable oil for frying

INSTRUCTIONS

Pat the chicken breasts dry with a paper towel. Using a sharp knife, score the breasts in a checkered pattern, meaning to make crosscuts across the breast, diagonally, to about half the thickness of the breast. We do this to expose the chicken to more seasoning and to make cooking faster and more even.

Season the chicken with a generous sprinkle of salt and lots of pepper, then rub the seasoning into all the crevasses.

Place a large skillet over medium-high heat, add enough vegetable oil to coat the bottom of the skillet, and heat the oil until it shimmers. Add the chicken, scored-side down. Cook for 3 to 4 minutes until browned, and flip. Cook for 3 to 4 minutes more until browned on the second side. Transfer to a plate and let cool for 2 to 3 minutes and you're ready to eat!

HERBY YOGURT SAUCE AND DIP

YIELD: SERVES 4

You will see a variation of these a lot in my recipes, so I thought I'd give them a formal introduction. I make simple yogurt-based dips and sauces because they're a much more nutritious alternative to other store-bought stuff and they also taste better. I use this as a base for poached eggs, a spread for sandwiches, and, most often, a dip for snacks.

INGREDIENTS

½ cup (120 g) full-fat plain Greek yogurt

¼ cup (weight varies) finely chopped fresh herbs (parsley, chives, cilantro)

1 garlic clove, minced

Juice of ½ lemon

INSTRUCTIONS

In a medium-size bowl, stir together all the ingredients using a whipping motion until incorporated. Refrigerate leftovers in an airtight container for up to 1 week.

PERFECT RICE EVERY TIME

YIELD: SERVES 2

Now, you may remember I told you to get a rice cooker. But, if you still don't have one, I'll try to save you with this easy way to make rice in a pot. Again, not as easy as a rice cooker, but still easy.

INGREDIENTS

1 cup (200 g) white rice (basmati, sushi rice)

1½ cups (360 ml) cold water

Pinch of kosher salt

INSTRUCTIONS

This first step is crucial, so don't skip it! Wash the rice in a fine-mesh sieve under a stream of cold water for 1 minute, making sure all the rice grains are thoroughly rinsed. This ensures the result is light and fluffy.

In a medium-size pot, combine the washed rice, cold water, and salt. Place the pot over high heat and bring to a boil. Once boiling, immediately turn the heat to the lowest setting and cover the pot with a lid. Simmer for 10 minutes and don't lift the lid!

Turn off the heat and move the pot away from the heat. Let the rice steam, with the lid on, for 5 to 10 minutes, depending on how patient you are.

Fluff with a fork and, boom, you've got perfectly cooked rice.

KWOOWK!

CHAPTER 2:

BREAKFAST TIME

I consider myself an advanced breakfast eater, and I am also very opinionated about it. These are some recipes that rank high on my breakfast scale.

FOOLPROOF BREAKFASTS

Superior Avocado Toast 32

Peanut Butter Banana
Baked Oats 35

Healthy(ish) Banana
Pancakes 36

Potato Breakfast Skillet
for One 38

Personal Power Smoothie 41

Custom Smoothie Bowls 42

GLOBAL BREAKFASTS

Swiss Bircher Muesli 44

Middle Eastern–Style
Shakshuka 47

EGG-CELLENT BREAKFASTS

Fully Loaded Omelet 48

Bacon, Avo, and Egg
Breakfast Tacos 51

My Special Shakshuka 52

Pro tip: *Most avocado toast recipes only require you to smash the avocado with a fork and add lime juice and salt. I respect that simplicity, but I take a more interesting approach and make something between an avocado salad and guacamole.*

SUPERIOR AVOCADO TOAST

YIELD: SERVES 1

The simple act of putting avocado on toast has come to define hipster eating across the world. And, some mornings, there's nothing better than the fatty goodness of avocado. Pair that with some toasted sourdough and barely cooked egg yolk dripping over it, and I'm ready to pay $18. Just kidding— we can make an even better version at home for a fraction of the cost. This recipe makes two slices, which is one portion for me, but if you prefer, give the other slice to your crush.

INSTRUCTIONS

Generously drizzle the bread slices with olive oil on both sides. Place a skillet big enough to hold both slices over medium-high heat, add the bread, and toast for about 4 minutes per side until golden brown.

In a large bowl, combine the avocado, tomato, shallot, garlic, lime juice and lime zest, herbs, and tahini. Using a fork, mix everything using a whipping motion (similar to beating eggs). This will break parts of the avocado and emulsify it with the tahini and lime juice, leading to a creamy, chunky texture variation. Taste and add some salt. Spread the avocado salad over the toast.

Top each toast with a soft-boiled egg (poached is overrated). Split the yolks and season with salt.

Pro tip: *To dice avocado, cut the avocado lengthwise around the pit and twist the two halves to open. Insert the knife into the pit by carefully hitting it, and pull out the pit with the help of the knife. Cut both halves into a checkered pattern, without cutting through the peel, then use a spoon to scoop out the diced flesh.*

INGREDIENTS

2 slices sourdough bread

Olive oil for drizzling

1 ripe avocado, diced (see Pro tip)

1 tomato, diced

½ shallot, finely diced

1 garlic clove, minced

Juice of ½ lime

Grated zest of ½ lime

1 small bunch fresh dill, finely chopped

1 small bunch fresh chives, finely chopped

1½ teaspoons tahini

Kosher salt

2 large soft-boiled eggs (see Boiled Eggs, the Easy Way, page 22)

PEANUT BUTTER BANANA BAKED OATS

YIELD: SERVES 4

I don't wanna be overly dramatic, but this recipe changed my life. I ate so much oatmeal one month that I think my blood might have been up to 1 percent oat milk! But, then I discovered this oat recipe that feels completely different. It's almost like banana bread, but healthier and more delicious. It melts in your mouth, and it has just the right level of sweetness, with a nice crunch. Plus, this recipe is ideal for meal prepping (the whole thing can be made in one baking dish) and it makes an easy-to-reheat breakfast or snack.

INGREDIENTS

1 ripe banana, plus ½ (optional)

1 large egg

¾ cup (180 ml) plant-based milk

1 tablespoon (16 g) peanut butter

1 tablespoon (15 g) full-fat plain Greek yogurt, plus more for topping

1½ teaspoons honey

1 cup (80 g) old-fashioned rolled oats

1 teaspoon ground cinnamon

1 teaspoon baking powder

½ teaspoon kosher salt

Handful of chopped walnuts

Handful of dried cranberries

INSTRUCTIONS

Preheat the oven to 350°F (180°C, or gas mark 4).

In a 9 × 13-inch (23 × 33 cm) glass baking dish, mash 1 ripe banana using a potato masher or a fork (or your clean hands, whatever).

Add the egg, milk, peanut butter, yogurt, and honey. These are your wet ingredients. Give them a whisk until the egg is beaten into the rest of the ingredients.

Add the dry ingredients: oats, cinnamon, baking powder, and salt. Whisk the mixture until well incorporated. It will have a (for lack of a better term) sloppy consistency.

This next step is highly customizable—add whatever mix-ins you prefer. I recommend chopped walnuts for a bit of crunch and dried cranberries for a tart but sweet addition. Stir those in.

Slice the remaining half banana (if using) and top the dish with those slices.

Bake for 40 minutes, or until the oatmeal is browned and crisp on top, but still moist on the inside.

Eat right away, while still warm, with a dollop of yogurt on top. Or, refrigerate in an airtight container for 2 to 3 days to have throughout the week. Reheating is easy in the microwave on medium-high power for about 1 minute.

HEALTHY(ISH) BANANA PANCAKES

YIELD: SERVES 1 OR 2

Look, I'm going to make a controversial statement, but don't tell anyone: I think pancakes are overrated. That's right, I said it. That was, until I tried these banana pancakes. The banana elevates the pancakes to a new, more exciting level for me. These pancakes are fluffy and moist, with multiple dimensions in flavor. After years of lazy Sunday mornings, I finally came up with a recipe that is more nutritious and easier to make than traditional pancakes. Because the ripe bananas have natural sugars in them, we only need a small amount of brown sugar to take these pancakes to a ten. Serve with sliced bananas, yogurt, or a drizzle of maple syrup.

INGREDIENTS

2 very ripe bananas

Pro tip: *If your bananas are not ripe, stick them, peeled, in a 350°F (180°C, or gas mark 4) oven for about 15 minutes until they turn black. They will now be ready to use for any baked dish.*

1 large egg

¾ cup (180 ml) milk

2 tablespoons (30 g) full-fat plain Greek yogurt

Splash of vanilla extract

1 cup (120 g) all-purpose flour

1 tablespoon (14 g) dark brown sugar

2 teaspoons baking powder

1 teaspoon ground cinnamon

½ teaspoon kosher salt

Butter for cooking

INSTRUCTIONS

In a large bowl, mash the bananas with a potato masher, fork, spoon, even your (clean) hands. It's okay to leave a few chunks.

Add the egg, milk, yogurt, and vanilla. Stir until everything is thoroughly incorporated with the bananas.

Add the flour, brown sugar, baking powder, cinnamon, and salt to the wet ingredients. Using a spatula, mix until just combined.

I prefer a lumpier, chunkier batter, which is why I recommend not overmixing everything.

Heat a large skillet or griddle over medium heat and add about 1 tablespoon (14 g) of butter to melt. Working in batches, using a ¼-cup or ⅓-cup measure, scoop the pancake batter into the hot pan. You should get 6 to 8 pancakes total. Cook for about 1½ minutes per side, depending on size, until cooked through and golden brown. All pancakes are different, so make sure to fine-tune the heat and cooking time for best results. Serve topped as you like.

POTATO BREAKFAST SKILLET FOR ONE

YIELD: SERVES 1

Sometimes I wake up on a weekend and decide to treat myself, although if you want to treat someone else, too, this recipe doubles easily (cook times stay the same). If the thought of warm egg yolk running down a bed of crispy bacon and cheesy potatoes, all topped with scallions and fresh herbs, intrigues you, give this recipe a shot. You don't have to thank me.

INGREDIENTS

3½ ounces (100 g) bacon, cut into bite-size pieces

½ white or yellow onion, finely diced

3 or 4 small red potatoes, cut into small dice

2 fresh jalapeño peppers, sliced, seeded for less heat

Kosher salt and ground black pepper

Finely chopped fresh sage leaves for garnish

2 large eggs

Handful of shredded cheddar or Gouda cheese

1 scallion, white and green parts, finely sliced

INSTRUCTIONS

Place the bacon into a medium-size cold skillet and place the skillet over medium-high heat. Cook for 4 to 5 minutes until the bacon is crispy and the fat has rendered. Use a slotted spoon to transfer the bacon to a paper towel to drain, leaving the bacon fat in the skillet.

Pro tip: *Starting with a cold skillet helps the bacon slowly release its fat without overcooking.*

Add the onion and cook for about 5 minutes until soft and fragrant. Add the potatoes and jalapeños.

Stir-fry for 1 minute, then add a splash of water. Cover the skillet with a lid and cook for about 10 minutes, giving everything a good stir every 2 minutes to ensure even cooking, until the potatoes are crispy on the outside and soft on the inside (like me!).

Season with salt (remember, the bacon is salty, so don't overdo it) and pepper to taste, then add chopped sage to taste and the cooked bacon. Give the ingredients a toss.

Using the back of a large wooden spoon or spatula, create 2 wells in the potatoes. Crack 1 egg into each well, trying not to break the yolks (crack the eggs on a flat surface). Season the eggs with salt and sprinkle the cheese over the dish. Add another splash of water, then re-cover the skillet and cook the eggs for 4 to 7 minutes, depending on preference, until the whites are set and the yolks still runny.

Top with sliced scallion and dig in straight out of the skillet because it's too delicious to wait any longer.

PERSONAL POWER SMOOTHIE

YIELD: SERVES 1

I really don't like it when people put the word "power" in front of dishes to give the illusion that the food has some sort of supernatural properties just because you put some fancy-sounding "health" powders in there.

That's marketing. That said, when I wake up after a night of having one too many cocktails (which I don't condone by the way), it does truly feel that this smoothie is giving me power (or at least reminding my body how to access it). There's nothing special about it: I just pack it with a wide array of micro and macronutrients, some electrolytes for hydration, and deliciousness for moral support. Hang in there!

When building your smoothie, keep some of these basic ingredients in mind, but also add your own according to your taste and needs. Some common add-ins for me are celery, frozen berries, Greek yogurt, peanut butter, oats, or cocoa powder.

INGREDIENTS

1 banana

1 small slice fresh ginger

Big handful of fresh spinach

1 cup (140 g) frozen pineapple chunks

Handful of raw almonds or cashews

1 cup (240 ml) coconut water

A few fresh mint leaves

INSTRUCTIONS

Simply combine all the ingredients in a blender and, well, blend. Adjust the amount of liquid according to your liking. Feel free to start with ½ cup (120 ml) of coconut water and determine the consistency from there.

Pro tip: *Turn this into a smoothie bowl by simply using less liquid for a much thicker consistency. Pour the smoothie into a bowl and top it with your favorite toppings, such as banana slices, chopped nuts, fresh blueberries, or oats.*

CUSTOM SMOOTHIE BOWLS

YIELD: SERVES 1

Instagram has changed the meaning of the word "smoothie" forever. What was once a humble blend of nutrient-rich breakfast ingredients has become a staple in any overpriced brunch restaurant's aesthetic feed. But, instead of paying too much for one, make it yourself, because beneath all the flashy looks, smoothie bowls should have a legitimate place in your breakfast game. You have ultimate control over the ingredients, which leads to a highly customizable experience.

The base smoothie is only the beginning (I slice leftover bananas and freeze them in freezer-safe bags for future smoothies and desserts). Because we're calling it a smoothie bowl, we have endless possibilities when it comes to toppings. I will show you three of my favorite variations but, using this simple method, craft your own smoothie bowl using your favorite ingredients.

INSTRUCTIONS

To make the smoothie base: All smoothie bowls start with the same foolproof base, and there's no need for ice. In a blender, combine the frozen banana slices, liquid of choice, and yogurt (if using; the yogurt adds nutrition and an extra creamy tang). Blend until smooth.

Pro tip: *For this next step, add anything you like, such as fruits and vegetables, grains, nuts, additional flavor and sweeteners, or even extra liquid to adjust the smoothie's thickness. Then, top with your favorite toppings.*

To make the green smoothie bowl: Make the smoothie base. Add the spinach and avocado to the base ingredients and blend

INGREDIENTS FOR SMOOTHIE BASE:

1 frozen banana, sliced

½ cup (120 ml) liquid (such as plant-based milk, fruit juice, coconut milk; I prefer coconut milk for its creaminess)

1 tablespoon (15 g) full-fat plain Greek yogurt (optional)

INGREDIENTS FOR GREEN SMOOTHIE BOWL:

1 cup (30 g) fresh spinach leaves

½ avocado, pitted

1 tablespoon (20 g) honey

1 teaspoon chia seeds

1 kiwi, peeled and sliced

INGREDIENTS FOR PB AND CHOCOLATE SMOOTHIE BOWL:

1 tablespoon (5 g) cocoa powder

1 tablespoon (16 g) peanut butter, plus more for garnish

1 tablespoon (20 g) maple syrup

1 tablespoon (5 g) old-fashioned rolled or quick-cooking oats

½ banana, sliced

1 tablespoon (8 g) grated dark chocolate

INGREDIENTS FOR CARROT CAKE SMOOTHIE BOWL:

½ cup (55 g) grated carrot

½ cup (40 g) old-fashioned rolled or quick-cooking oats

½ cup (120 ml) carrot juice

1 teaspoon maple syrup

1 teaspoon ground cinnamon, plus ½ teaspoon

1 teaspoon ground nutmeg

¼ cup (30 g) chopped walnuts

¼ cup (20 g) coconut flakes

until smooth. Pour the smoothie into a bowl. Drizzle with the honey, sprinkle with chia seeds, and top with kiwi to serve.

To make the PB and chocolate smoothie bowl: Make the smoothie base. Add the cocoa powder, peanut butter, and maple syrup to the base ingredients and blend until smooth. Pour the smoothie into a bowl. Sprinkle with the oats, then top with the banana, chocolate, and a spoonful of peanut butter to serve.

To make the carrot cake smoothie bowl: Make the smoothie base. Add the carrot, oats, carrot juice, maple syrup, 1 teaspoon of cinnamon, and nutmeg to the base ingredients and blend until smooth. Pour the smoothie into a bowl. Sprinkle with the walnuts, coconut, and remaining ½ teaspoon of cinnamon to serve.

Take an Instagram picture and watch the likes come in. Alternatively, you could mindfully appreciate your smoothie bowl, without becoming addicted to the tiny but constant dopamine release caused by every single online notification (trust me, I've been there).

SWISS BIRCHER MUESLI

YIELD: SERVES 1

More than 150 years ago, this guy named Dr. Bircher-Benner, a Swiss physician, invented this dish to serve to his patients as part of a healthy, nutrient-rich diet. Little did he know, he was about to change the world of breakfast forever, including my own. I eat a variation of this breakfast virtually every day. It packs so much nutritional value, and it provides an ideal combination of taste and texture. A lot of people soak their oats overnight; however, I find that even a 10-minute soak leads to a delicious and convenient breakfast.

INSTRUCTIONS

To make the muesli: In a large bowl, stir together the oats, milk, apple juice, apple, cranberries, peanut butter, yogurt, and 1 teaspoon of honey. The order or technique doesn't matter, as long as everything is thoroughly mixed and incorporated. Adjust the milk based on your texture preference; keep in mind the oats will absorb most of the liquid. This step is highly customizable—feel free to include any mix-ins you prefer.

Let the muesli sit for 5 to 10 minutes and your oats should be ready (most days for me it's closer to 5 minutes).

To make the toasted almond flakes: While the oats sit, in a small dry skillet over medium heat, combine the almond flakes (feel free to use other nuts; sometimes I go for chopped walnuts or pecans) and cinnamon. Toast for 3 to 4 minutes, stirring constantly, until fragrant and slightly browned. Remove from the heat.

Transfer the soaked oats to a bowl. Top with the almond flakes and berries and a drizzle of honey (if using).

INGREDIENTS FOR MUESLI:

½ cup (40 g) old-fashioned rolled oats

½ cup (120 ml) milk of choice (I use oat milk), plus more as needed

Splash of apple juice

½ Granny Smith apple, grated

Handful of dried cranberries

1 tablespoon (16 g) peanut butter

1 tablespoon (15 g) full-fat plain Greek yogurt

1 teaspoon honey, plus more for drizzling (optional)

INGREDIENTS FOR TOASTED ALMOND FLAKES:

Generous handful of almond flakes or sliced almonds

1 teaspoon ground cinnamon

Mixed fresh berries for topping (I like raspberries, blueberries, blackberries, or a mix).

MIDDLE EASTERN–STYLE SHAKSHUKA

YIELD: SERVES 2

Shakshuka is one of those breakfast dishes I go back to repeatedly, and every time I do, I'm reminded how much I love it. It's a filling, hearty dish, and it elevates every ingredient to something special. Picture a slice of sourdough breaking into a gently poached egg surrounded by a spicy tomato sauce, all topped with fresh herbs and cheese. Pretty much breakfast perfection. The origin of the dish is unclear, but it is widely spread throughout North Africa and very popular in the Middle East, and it's now going to be on your table, because you have to make this as soon as possible. Thank me later.

INGREDIENTS

1 tablespoon (15 ml) olive oil

1 yellow onion, diced

1 red bell pepper, diced

1 fresh green chile (such as serrano), sliced, seeded for less heat

2 garlic cloves, crushed

1 teaspoon cumin seeds

1 teaspoon paprika

½ teaspoon chili powder

Kosher salt

1 (14-ounce, or 395 g) can crushed tomatoes

3 or 4 large eggs

Crumbled feta cheese for topping

1 bunch fresh parsley, chopped

Sourdough bread for serving (optional)

INSTRUCTIONS

Coat a large skillet with the oil and place it over medium heat. Add the onion and bell pepper. Sauté for 5 to 6 minutes, stirring occasionally, until the onion becomes translucent and the bell pepper has softened. Add the green chile, garlic, cumin seeds, paprika, and chili powder. (I add the salt later, to better control the salt level in the final dish.) Sauté for a couple of minutes until you can smell the aromatics and spices coming together.

Add the crushed tomatoes to the skillet. Simmer for 3 to 4 minutes, stirring. Taste the sauce and add enough salt to bring out the flavors.

Using the back of a large wooden spoon or spatula, create 3 or 4 small wells in the sauce. Carefully crack 1 egg into each well, trying not to break the yolks (crack the eggs on a flat surface). Cover the skillet with a lid and cook for 5 to 7 minutes until the egg whites are set, or to your preferred doneness. The yolks should still be runny.

Turn off the heat and top the shakshuka with feta cheese and chopped parsley. I serve shakshuka with sourdough bread for dipping into the eggs and delicious sauce.

FULLY LOADED OMELET

YIELD: SERVES 1

The classic omelet is both elegant and simple, and with proper technique, it can be luxurious. However, I'm a fan of adding a few extra things, for flavor, nutritional value, and, well, fun. I see the omelet as a blank canvas waiting to receive exciting ingredients of my choice. This recipe is a great way to use up any leftover or forgotten vegetables in your fridge, so feel free to customize it to what you have or like.

INGREDIENTS

1 tablespoon (15 ml) olive oil

½ cup (55 g) diced smoked chorizo

2 scallions, white and green parts, sliced, separated

Handful of chestnut mushrooms, sliced

2 large eggs

Kosher salt

Grated Gouda or cheddar cheese for topping

½ avocado, pitted and sliced

Sour cream for topping

Chopped fresh cilantro for topping

INSTRUCTIONS

Place a small skillet or omelet pan over medium heat and swirl in the oil to coat the pan. Add the chorizo and cook for about 4 minutes until some of the fat has rendered and the chorizo has a crispy appearance. Add the scallion whites and cook with the chorizo no longer than 2 minutes until the scallion turns soft and fragrant. Add the mushrooms. Don't worry if it seems like mushroom overload; they shrink a lot during cooking. Cook for 2 to 3 minutes until soft and reduced roughly by half in size.

In a small bowl or mug, whisk the eggs and pour them into the skillet. If you hear too much sizzling when the eggs hit the pan,

lower the heat slightly—eggs require a lot of care and attention when it comes to the heat level. As soon as the eggs hit the pan, keep them moving gently using a rubber spatula. Pick up some of the cooked egg that has settled at the bottom with every movement to cook the eggs evenly. You don't want an overcooked bottom and raw egg on top. Do this until the omelet settles (when you feel you can't move it anymore without tearing it).

Season with salt to taste, and sprinkle some grated cheese on the omelet. Turn the heat to medium-low, cover the skillet with a lid, and cook for another minute until the cheese melts. Transfer your omelet to a plate.

This is my favorite part: Top your omelet with avocado slices, a dollop of sour cream, and a sprinkle of fresh cilantro (or parsley). Sometimes, I add tomato, too.

BACON, AVO, AND EGG BREAKFAST TACOS

YIELD: SERVES 1

I once took my girlfriend to Sunday brunch to this place we'd never been. They had great coffee, and the people sitting there looked pretty cool, so I thought: *For sure their breakfast is great!* We were starving and ordered breakfast tacos. I was picturing a lovely, soft, slightly charred corn tortilla, creamy scrambled eggs, silky avocado, and a bit of salty bacon. BUT, what we got was NOT that. I'm not kidding. The waiter came out with one cold grocery store crispy tortilla with overcooked eggs inside and that was it! I was too shy to complain and just ate it in sadness. But, when I got home, I made the recipe I truly wanted, and guess what? It was also a fraction of the price. Here is that recipe.

INGREDIENTS

1 avocado, peeled, halved, and pitted

Juice of ½ lime

Kosher salt

2 thick-cut bacon slices

1½ teaspoons butter

2 large eggs

1 teaspoon full-fat plain Greek yogurt

2 (4- or 6-inch, 10 or 15 cm) corn tortillas

Red pepper flakes for topping

Chopped fresh cilantro for topping

INSTRUCTIONS

In a small bowl, smash the avocado with a fork, leaving some chunks. Stir in the lime juice and salt to taste and you've got a simply delicious avocado spread.

Pro tip: *To master the avocado, see Superior Avocado Toast, Pro tip, page 32.*

Place the bacon in a medium-size cold skillet and place the skillet over medium heat. Cook the bacon for 3 to 4 minutes per side until crispy, making sure the fat has rendered. Transfer the bacon to a cutting board, leaving the bacon fat in the skillet. Chop the bacon into bite-size pieces.

Return the skillet with the bacon grease to medium heat and add the butter to melt.

In a small bowl, whisk the eggs and yogurt to blend, then add the eggs to the skillet. Turn the heat to medium-low and stir constantly and fairly vigorously. We want a soft scramble here, soft curds that almost melt into the thick liquid egg around them—they need to be spoonable.

The eggs cook quickly, so while stirring, pay attention to consistency. Turn off the heat and pull the eggs to one side of the skillet just before they're fully cooked. They will continue to cook from the residual heat.

In another skillet over high heat, warm the tortillas for 15 to 20 seconds per side.

Now, fill them: Start with the scrambled eggs, then spread the avocado on top. Complete with the bacon, red pepper flakes, and cilantro.

MY SPECIAL SHAKSHUKA

YIELD: SERVES 2

If you know me (or tried the Middle Eastern–Style Shakshuka on page 47), you know I hold shakshuka in a special place in my breakfast heart. I've developed tweaks that, in my opinion, dramatically improve the dish's taste and nutritional value, adding extra vegetables, some lovely chickpeas, and unexpected flavor enhancers that take shakshuka to a ten. What I love most, though, is that you can use any leftovers forgotten in the back of your fridge, and this dish elevates them. Serve with bread for dipping, if you like.

INSTRUCTIONS

Swirl the oil in a large skillet to coat and place it over medium heat. Add the onion, garlic, green chile, and cumin seeds—the aromatics. Cook for 4 to 5 minutes, stirring to prevent burning, until fragrant and the onion is translucent.

Add the bell pepper, eggplant, and chickpeas. Sprinkle evenly with a generous pinch of salt, which will draw out some of the eggplant's moisture and help the cooking process. Cook for 5 to 8 minutes, depending on the size of your eggplant pieces, stirring occasionally, until tender but not mushy. The eggplant will lose its raw edge and develop a meaty, tender, melty texture. To speed this up, cover the skillet with a lid. Don't be afraid to taste the eggplant to determine whether it's cooked.

Stir in the paprika and turmeric (if using), then the crushed tomatoes. Simmer the sauce for 3 to 5 minutes until thickened slightly. Taste and season with salt, as needed.

Using the back of a large wooden spoon or spatula, create 3 or 4 small wells in the sauce. Carefully crack 1 egg into each well, trying not to break the yolks (crack the eggs on a flat surface). Cover the skillet with a lid and simmer over medium heat for 5 to 7 minutes until the egg whites are set, or to your desired doneness. The yolks should still be runny. Remove from the heat. Top with feta and fresh parsley to serve.

Pro tip: *Gently poke the eggs to assess doneness. If the whites feel too liquid-y, cook them a bit longer until they develop a gentle firmness. You can also assess the softness of the yolk, since you don't want it to firm up.*

INGREDIENTS

1 tablespoon (15 ml) olive oil

½ yellow onion, thinly sliced

2 garlic cloves

1 fresh hot green chile (such as serrano), sliced, seeded for less heat

1 teaspoon cumin seeds

1 green bell pepper, diced

¾ cup (62 g) small dice eggplant

½ (15-ounce, or 425 g) can chickpeas, drained (save the remainder for another use)

Kosher salt

1 teaspoon paprika

½ teaspoon ground turmeric (optional)

1 (14-ounce, or 395 g) can crushed tomatoes

3 or 4 large eggs

Crumbled feta cheese for topping

1 bunch fresh parsley, chopped

CHAPTER 3:

ON THE GO OR AT THE DESK

No BS. Nutritious, efficient, and enjoyable food.
Simple as that.

HANDHELD MEALS

My Triple-Decker Chicken Sandwich	56
Healthy Buffalo Chicken Pita	59
Chickpea Wrap	60
Tastiest Chicken Lunch Wrap	63
Tuna Melt Quesadilla	64

SALADS

The Gourmet Egg Salad Bagel	67
Crispy Chickpea Sweet Potato Salad	68
My Ultimate Chicken Taco Salad	71
Mediterranean Pasta Salad	75
Fresh Summer Quinoa Salad	76

MY TRIPLE-DECKER CHICKEN SANDWICH

YIELD: SERVES 1

In middle school, my mom always packed a sandwich for my lunch. They were always wrapped in a colorful napkin and were so good, unusually good for a sandwich. She told me she had a secret "love" spice in her pantry, and I was always looking for it. Come to think of it, she probably made it up. Anyway, this sandwich is inspired by that, and it's one of my go-to quick lunches. And because I can do whatever I want, I make it a triple decker, for an extra layer of fun. I usually use leftover chicken breast (see Straightforward Chicken Breast, page 25) for this, but here I show you how to make a special black pepper lemon chicken that enhances this sandwich.

INSTRUCTIONS

To make the chicken for the sandwich: In case you don't have leftover chicken, make this easy black pepper lemon chicken breast: Using a sharp knife, butterfly the chicken breast (cut through the middle of the chicken breast, horizontally, using a sawing motion, stopping right before cutting all the way through, and then open the chicken breast like a book; see page 18 for more). Season the chicken with salt and pepper (go heavy with the pepper), and sprinkle it with lemon juice. Use your clean hands to rub the lemon juice and the seasonings into the chicken.

Pour enough oil into a medium-size skillet to coat the skillet, place it over medium-high heat, and heat the olive oil until it shimmers. Add the chicken. Cook for 3 minutes per side until gently browned. Transfer the chicken to a cutting board and let rest for 5 minutes, then cut the chicken into bite-size slices (I cut my pieces on the thinner side because I like to layer them). Sprinkle the chicken with lemon zest, making sure to coat every piece.

To make the sauce: In a small bowl, combine the yogurt, tahini, garlic, lemon zest, lemon juice, and olive oil. Season with dill and salt to taste. Whisk until combined. Nothing fancy here.

To assemble the sandwich: Make sure your bread is toasted and start with the bottom slice. Spread one-third of the sauce onto the bottom piece of toast, top with half the salted tomato slices, half the black pepper lemon chicken pieces, and a handful of fresh arugula. Continue with the next slice of toast, spreading it with one-third of the sauce and stacking the ingredients the same way. Before adding the final slice of toast, spread it with the remaining sauce and place it sauce-side down to finish the sandwich.

Cut the sandwich into 2 triangles (or don't) and serve.

INGREDIENTS FOR CHICKEN SANDWICH:

1 boneless, skinless chicken breast

Kosher salt and freshly cracked black pepper

Juice of ½ lemon

Olive oil for cooking

Grated zest of ½ lemon

3 slices sandwich bread of choice, toasted

1 tomato, sliced and salted

2 handfuls of fresh arugula

INGREDIENTS FOR SAUCE:

2 tablespoons (30 g) full-fat plain Greek yogurt

1½ teaspoons tahini

1 or 2 garlic cloves, minced

Grated zest of ½ lemon

Juice of ½ lemon

1 teaspoon olive oil

Chopped fresh dill for seasoning

Kosher salt

HEALTHY BUFFALO CHICKEN PITA

YIELD: SERVES 1

This is one of my favorite weekday macro-friendly recipes, meaning it's got some useful nutrients and not a lot of calories, which makes it appropriate for weight loss, if that's your thing. It takes very little effort, and the result is ridiculously satisfying. I use chicken breast and, after cooking it, coat it with a buffalo-inspired sauce, creating a juicy, sweet, hot, and savory experience, all wrapped in a warm pita. I usually enjoy this sandwich with a fresh garlic yogurt dip, but even by itself, this handheld dish is one you will come back to many times—I promise.

INGREDIENTS

1 boneless, skinless chicken breast

1 teaspoon smoked paprika

1 teaspoon garlic powder

Kosher salt and ground black pepper

Olive oil for cooking

1 tablespoon (15 g) full-fat plain Greek yogurt

1 tablespoon (15 ml) hot sauce (I like Frank's RedHot Buffalo Wings sauce), plus more as needed

1 teaspoon honey

1 scallion, white and green parts, sliced

1 small bunch fresh cilantro, roughly chopped

1 medium-size pita bread

Handful of grated Gouda or cheddar cheese

INSTRUCTIONS

Preheat the oven to 350°F (180°C, or gas mark 4).

Now, let's take care of the chicken breast. Cut it into bite-size pieces.

Pro tip: *I prefer smaller pieces because they cook faster and the sauce-to-meat ratio is better.*

Season the chicken with the paprika and garlic powder and then with salt and pepper to taste. Make sure the seasonings thoroughly coat all the chicken pieces.

Pour enough oil into a 12-inch (30 cm) skillet to coat the skillet, place it over medium-high heat, and heat the oil until it shimmers. Add the chicken and cook for 5 to 6 minutes, flipping the pieces throughout to make sure all sides are properly cooked. Transfer the cooked chicken to a large bowl.

Stir in the yogurt, hot sauce, honey, scallion, and cilantro until thoroughly mixed and all the chicken is coated. Taste one piece and add more salt, pepper, or hot sauce, as needed.

Cut off a small edge piece from the pita bread, and using that opening, cut through the pita bread, stopping before cutting all the way through, to completely open it up like a pocket for the filling.

Stuff the pita with the chicken mixture and top with some grated cheese. Place the pita on a baking sheet.

Bake for about 5 minutes, or until the cheese melts. Let cool until it's comfortable to handle.

CHICKPEA WRAP

YIELD: SERVES 1

A lot of people make fun of me for always using chickpeas in my recipes, and my daily life. At first, I tried to defend myself and deny my chickpea obsession, but I've since come to accept that this is who I am: I am a chickpea man. These herbed-up chickpeas are my go-to chickpea meal, and they're so versatile you can use them in anything. Lately, I've been reworking this chickpea wrap that cuts through the herby, garlicky intensity of the chickpeas with some yogurt. Plus, it's handheld and mess-free. What's not to love?

INSTRUCTIONS

Pour the oil into a 12-inch (30 cm) skillet, place the skillet over medium heat, and heat the oil until it shimmers. Add the chickpeas and give them a toss in the hot oil. Add the garlic, all the dried herbs and spices, and season with salt and pepper to taste, ensuring the seasonings coat the chickpeas completely. Cook for 10 to 12 minutes, stirring and tossing occasionally, until the chickpeas develop a crispy outside and a soft inside (carefully, they're hot; try one to see).

Turn off the heat and add the fresh herbs. This recipe is herb heavy, so don't be afraid to add a good amount—it's hard to overdo it, in my opinion. As long as the stars of the show are still the chickpeas, and not the herbs, you're good. Add the red chile and lemon juice and stir until everything is incorporated.

Place a clean, dry skillet over medium heat. Add the tortilla wrap and warm carefully for just a few seconds. We're not toasting here, just warming: This will help the pliability. Transfer to a work surface. Spread the yogurt over the tortilla with a spoon. Top with the chickpeas and wrap it up (see Folding a Burrito, page 20).

INGREDIENTS

1 tablespoon (15 ml) olive oil

½ (15-ounce, or 425 g) can chickpeas, drained and rinsed (to prevent too much of the starchy coating from sticking to the pan; save the remainder for another use)

2 or 3 garlic cloves, sliced

1 teaspoon ground cumin

1 teaspoon smoked paprika

1 teaspoon dried thyme

1 teaspoon garlic powder

Kosher salt and ground black pepper

1 bunch fresh herbs (I like cilantro and parsley)

1 fresh red chile, sliced, seeded for less heat

Juice of ½ lemon

1 (12-inch, or 30 cm) tortilla wrap

1 tablespoon (15 g) full-fat plain Greek yogurt

TASTIEST CHICKEN LUNCH WRAP

YIELD: SERVES 1

This dish has everything I need from a wrap: convenience, quality nutrients, and fun. The juiciest chicken, a rich sauce, some veggie crunch, and a little acidic kick all come together into this tightly packed lunch wrap. You can totally use leftover chicken for this, but to get the full experience, make these juicy chicken thigh bites right before using so you can eat them hot and fresh.

INSTRUCTIONS

To prepare the chicken, cut the thigh into small bite-size pieces and transfer them to a medium-size bowl. Add the garlic, salt and pepper to taste, paprika, garlic powder, and turmeric. (The earthy, peppery turmeric flavor works very well in this recipe). Sprinkle in the lemon juice, then give everything a stir until the chicken is well coated with the spices and the garlic and lemon juice is distributed thoroughly. You can cover this and let it marinate in the fridge for a couple of hours for the maximum experience, but if I'm being honest, 99 percent of the time I just cook it right away.

Pour about 1 tablespoon (15 ml) of olive oil into a 12-inch (30 cm) skillet, place the skillet over medium-high heat, and heat the oil until it shimmers. Add the chicken to the hot oil and cook for 5 to 6 minutes, stirring occasionally, until a nice golden-brown color is achieved.

In a small bowl, stir together the yogurt, mayo, and cilantro until blended.

Place the warmed tortilla on a work surface and spread half the sauce over it. Add the chicken, bunching it toward the center of the wrap. Top the chicken with the tomato and red cabbage. Dollop the rest of the sauce on top and finish with some pickled onion slices. Wrap up your tortilla (see Folding a Burrito, page 20) and celebrate your success.

INGREDIENTS

1 boneless, skinless chicken thigh

1 garlic clove, minced

Kosher salt and ground black pepper

1 teaspoon smoked paprika

1 teaspoon garlic powder

1 teaspoon ground turmeric

Juice of ½ lemon

Olive oil for cooking

1 tablespoon (15 g) full-fat plain Greek yogurt

1½ teaspoons mayonnaise

1 small bunch fresh cilantro, chopped

1 (12-inch, or 30 cm) flour tortilla wrap, warmed

½ tomato, diced and salted

Handful of chopped red cabbage

Pickled red onions (See Pickled Red Onions and Other Things, page 24) for topping

TUNA MELT QUESADILLA

YIELD: SERVES 1

Sometimes, you look into your fridge and it seems as though you have nothing to eat. Plus, you're too lazy to go to the store and take-out is too expensive. When I'm in that situation, this dish always comes through. These are common ingredients to keep on hand: a can of tuna, a tortilla wrap, spices and condiments, some leftover cheese. Although these ingredients don't sound too flashy, when you put them together into this tuna melt quesadilla, you'll feel like you created something from nothing.

INSTRUCTIONS

Place the drained tuna can into a small bowl. Add the mayo, red onion, garlic, parsley, and capers. Using a fork, mix until thoroughly incorporated. Add the olive oil and mix until the tuna mixture is completely emulsified. The oil contributes to a richer experience. The salad should look almost paste-like. Season with salt and pepper to taste.

Place the tortilla on a work surface and spread the tuna on half of the tortilla only (you will need to fold it). Add enough shredded cheddar to cover the tuna completely, then fold the other side on top of the tuna. Gently press down on the tortilla to fix it in place.

Heat a large skillet or a griddle over medium-high heat. Add a little bit of oil and spread it out, making sure it coats the cooking surface. Once hot, place the quesadilla in the skillet, cheese-side down. Brush the top side with some more oil to coat the tortilla and let it cook for 2 to 3 minutes. You can check the bottom for some browning, but make sure not to burn it. Carefully flip the tortilla and cook for 2 minutes more until browned.

That's it! Take it out and cut it into three triangles.

INGREDIENTS

½ (5-ounce, or 140 g) can water-packed tuna, drained

2 tablespoons (30 g) mayonnaise

½ red onion, finely diced

1 garlic clove, minced

1 small bunch fresh parsley, roughly chopped

1 tablespoon (9 g) capers, drained

1 tablespoon (15 ml) olive oil, plus more for cooking

Kosher salt and ground black pepper

1 (10-inch, or 25 cm) flour tortilla wrap

Handful of grated cheddar cheese

THE GOURMET EGG SALAD BAGEL

YIELD: SERVES 2

When I say "egg salad," you might think of bad airport sandwiches that somehow manage to be both mushy and dry, lacking any depth of flavor. But, I invite you to open your mind, because the humble egg salad can be an extremely satisfying and flavorful experience if done right, and it's also affordable! You can double this recipe and refrigerate it for up to five days. I eat this on a sesame seed bagel; you can also wrap it in lettuce leaves.

INSTRUCTIONS

Pro tip: *This recipe is straightforward, but you do need some boiled eggs before starting. Although you can purchase hard-boiled eggs at the store, I recommend not completely hard-boiling the eggs, so cooking them yourself gives you that control. A slightly soft yolk greatly increases the texture of the egg salad. The ideal cook time on the eggs is 8 minutes for me.*

Peel the eggs and place them in a large bowl. Add the mayo, yogurt, Dijon, vinegar, celery, and all the fresh herbs. Season to taste with salt and pepper. Start lightly with the salt since you can add more to the finished product. Also add the olive oil to enhance the richness of the salad.

Using your very clean hands, roughly mash the eggs and mix them with the other ingredients. I find using my hands gives me the texture variation I love, not to mention it's incredibly fun. We're going for a chunky, but still creamy and held together, consistency.

If you like (I like!), preheat the oven to 350°F (180°C, or gas mark 4). Place the bagel halves on a baking sheet and warm for about 3 minutes.

Pile the egg salad on the bagel halves and get ready for your mind to be changed about egg salad.

INGREDIENTS

4 large hard-boiled eggs (see Boiled Eggs, the Easy Way, page 22)

¼ cup (60 g) light or regular mayonnaise

2 tablespoons (30 g) full-fat plain Greek yogurt

1½ teaspoons Dijon mustard

1 teaspoon white vinegar

1 small celery stalk, finely chopped

1 tablespoon (4 g) chopped fresh dill

1 tablespoon (4 g) chopped fresh parsley

1 tablespoon (3 g) chopped fresh chives

Kosher salt and ground black pepper

1 tablespoon (15 ml) olive oil

Sesame seed bagel, halved

CRISPY CHICKPEA SWEET POTATO SALAD

YIELD: SERVES 2

Throughout this book you'll notice my (borderline unhealthy) obsession with certain ingredients. One that you may have already picked up on is chickpeas, and another that I'm introducing now is sweet potatoes. Not only do these two ingredients form an incredibly nutritionally complex food combo, but they also taste delicious together. This salad makes them the star and elevates them with a simple garlicky dressing.

I'll also tell you that the term "salad," in my mind, is loosely defined. I'm not a fan of leaf-heavy salads. I think they're a useful addition to a salad, but I don't think they should be what defines it. I want a variety of colors, tastes, textures, fats, acids, and aromatics, all contributing to an exciting experience. When I learned to think outside the box with salads, I stopped hating them and started incorporating them into my daily diet. So, leave your preconceived ideas about what a salad is at the previous page, and explore these recipes with an open mind.

INGREDIENTS FOR SPICE MIX:

Kosher salt, to taste

2 teaspoons smoked paprika

2 teaspoons ground cumin

2 teaspoons garlic powder

1 teaspoon ground ginger

INGREDIENTS FOR CRISPY CHICKPEAS:

1 (15-ounce, or 425 g) can chickpeas, drained, rinsed, and dried

1 tablespoon (15 ml) olive oil

INGREDIENTS FOR SWEET POTATO:

1 tablespoon olive oil

1 medium-size sweet potato, cut into small dice

1 small bunch fresh parsley, roughly chopped

INSTRUCTIONS

To make the spice mix: In a small bowl, stir together all the spices.

Preheat the oven to 400°F (200°C, or gas mark 6). Line a sheet pan with parchment paper.

To make the crispy chickpeas: In a medium-size bowl, combine the dried chickpeas, olive oil, and half the spice mix. Using a wooden spoon, stir the chickpeas until they're thoroughly coated with the spice mix. Spread the chickpeas on the prepared sheet pan, making sure there aren't any big clusters.

INGREDIENTS FOR DRESSING:

¼ cup (60 g) full-fat plain Greek yogurt

2 tablespoons (30 g) tahini

2 or 3 garlic cloves, peeled (I always go for 3)

1 medium-size bunch fresh cilantro

Grated zest of 1 lime

Juice of 1 lime

1 tablespoon (15 ml) olive oil

2 teaspoons honey

Kosher salt and ground black pepper

INGREDIENTS FOR SALAD:

2 or 3 handfuls of any leafy greens (I use corn salad [mâche])

Bake for 20 to 30 minutes until the chickpeas are crispy on the outside. Check on them periodically to make sure they don't burn.

Pro tip: *I make my sweet potato straight in a skillet. It's more convenient and I feel like it leads to a better texture.*

To make the sweet potato: Pour the oil into a large skillet to coat, place the skillet over medium-high heat, and heat the oil until it shimmers. Add the sweet potato. Cook for about 1 minute, tossing, then turn the heat to medium. Spread the sweet potato in the skillet so each piece is in contact with the cooking surface. Add a big splash of water to the pan and immediately cover it with a lid. This will steam the sweet potato while also giving the pieces a bit of a crispy exterior. Cook the sweet potato like this for 10 to 15 minutes, depending on how big your pieces are. Every 2 minutes, lift the lid and give everything a stir to ensure even cooking. To see if the sweet potato is done, carefully taste a small piece.

When the sweet potato is done, maintain the medium heat and stir in the remaining spice mix, distributing it evenly. Toss and stir to coat all the sweet potato pieces, then stir in the chopped parsley and turn off the heat.

To make the dressing: In a food processor or a blender, combine all the dressing ingredients, including salt and pepper to taste, and process until smooth. Use small amounts of water to thin the dressing, depending on your preference. Taste and season with more salt and pepper, as needed.

To assemble the salad: In a large bowl, combine the leafy greens, sweet potato, and crispy chickpeas. Toss with a small amount of dressing to coat and combine. Gradually increase the amount of dressing to taste, making sure not to overdress the salad. You don't want the salad to be soggy.

Refrigerate leftover dressing in a small covered jar or a squirt bottle for up to 1 week.

MY ULTIMATE CHICKEN TACO SALAD

YIELD: SERVES 2

I'm going to be honest with you: This is my favorite salad in this chapter, actually one of my favorite dishes in the book. I make this recipe at least once a week, and I'm always left satisfied. My salad philosophy is that the best salads take tried-and-tested flavor profiles from other dishes and convert them into salad format. That is what this salad is for me. Chicken tacos are one of my favorite foods: I think they balance nutrition and fun. With this salad, I combine all the ingredients I use to make chicken tacos, but create a salad instead, with a very special salad dressing, and some spicy tortilla "croutons" for that satisfying crunch.

INSTRUCTIONS

To make the dressing: In a blender, combine all the dressing ingredients and blend until thick and creamy. If it's too thick, add small splashes of water until it reaches your desired consistency.

To make the salad: Using a sharp knife, butterfly the chicken breast (see page 18 for more). Season the chicken generously with the taco seasoning, just enough to coat it. You won't use the whole packet here—we'll need some later.

Pour 1 tablespoon (15 ml) of olive oil into a 12-inch (30 cm) skillet, place the skillet over medium-high heat, and heat the oil until it shimmers. Add the chicken and cook for about 3 minutes per side until gently browned. Without turning off the heat, transfer the chicken to a plate and let rest for 2 minutes. Cut the chicken into bite-size pieces.

Add a touch more oil to the skillet, still over medium-high heat. Add the tortilla ribbons and cook for 5 minutes, tossing occasionally, until they're slightly crispy. Sprinkle with some more taco seasoning

INGREDIENTS FOR DRESSING:

1 avocado, peeled, halved, and pitted

1 tablespoon (15 g) full-fat plain Greek yogurt

1 tablespoon (15 ml) olive oil

Grated zest of 1 lime

Juice of 1 lime

1 garlic clove

Kosher salt and ground black pepper

INGREDIENTS FOR SALAD:

1 boneless, skinless chicken breast

1 (1-ounce, or 28 g) packet taco seasoning

Olive oil for cooking

2 or 3 small (6-inch, or 15 cm) flour tortillas, thinly sliced into ribbons

1 head baby romaine lettuce, roughly chopped

½ ear fresh corn, kernels cut from the cob

1 scallion, white and green parts, sliced

2 Roma tomatoes, diced

1 bunch fresh cilantro, roughly chopped

and toss until coated. Cook for 1 minute and turn off the heat. These are our "croutons."

In a large bowl, combine all the fresh ingredients: the lettuce, corn, scallion, tomatoes, and cilantro. Add the chicken and tortilla ribbons and give everything a toss. Add your desired amount of dressing and toss until everything is coated and combined.

THE SALAD DRESSING FORMULA

A salad dressing makes or breaks a salad. The beauty of dressings is that you have ultimate control over their taste and nutritional value. As long as you stick to this basic principle, you're guaranteed quality salad dressings every time.

The formula:

1 Part Oil/Fat + 1 Part Acid + Aromatics + Flavor/Texture/Nutrition Enhancers

Use 1 part of an oil or fat, like olive oil or avocado oil, with 1 part of an acid of choice, like white wine vinegar or fresh lemon juice, for the base emulsion.

Aromatics are added to create strong flavors in the dressing: think garlic, herbs, even things like sun-dried tomatoes.

Then, you can pretty much add whatever you want to enhance the flavor, texture, or nutritional value of your dressing: Some of my favorite add-ins are avocado, Greek yogurt, honey, maple syrup, mustard, and, of course, salt and pepper.

Use this formula to experiment with different flavor profiles for different types of salads. Think of your favorite dishes and break down some base ingredients you can use in a dressing. After that, experiment with add-ins. Eventually, you'll end up with your favorite salad dressing, one that you created yourself.

MEDITERRANEAN PASTA SALAD

YIELD: SERVES 2

Get this: A salad does not need leafy greens. You can get very creative with your salad bases, and one of my favorites is pasta. Let's be honest, pasta is objectively more enjoyable than leaves, so why not build your salad on top of it? This dish makes a great lunch—it's fresh, easy to make, but also hearty and satisfying. Plus, the Mediterranean-inspired ingredients create a light, summery experience, along with the lemony bite of the simple vinaigrette.

INSTRUCTIONS

To make the dressing: In a small jar with a lid, combine the dressing ingredients, including salt and pepper to taste. Seal the lid and give the jar a good shake until everything is emulsified and homogenous. Taste the dressing and adjust the seasoning as needed: It should be saltier and more acidic than you think, because its bite will decrease in the final dish.

To make the salad: Cook the pasta in a large pot of salted water according to the package directions until al dente. Drain and rinse under cold water, then transfer the cooked pasta to a large bowl. Pour in the oil and give the pasta a toss to coat. Add the parsley and toss again until evenly distributed.

Add the tomatoes, onion, cucumber, feta, olives, and capers. Pour on a small amount of dressing and give everything a toss to coat and combine. Taste and add more dressing, as needed.

Refrigerate any leftover dressing, covered, for up to 2 weeks.

INGREDIENTS FOR DRESSING:

2 tablespoons (30 ml) red wine vinegar

2 tablespoons (30 ml) olive oil

Grated zest of ½ lemon

Juice of ½ lemon, plus more as needed

Sprinkle of fresh thyme leaves

Kosher salt and ground black pepper

INGREDIENTS FOR SALAD:

4 ounces (115 g) dried pasta of choice (I like farfalle)

1 tablespoon (15 ml) olive oil

Big handful of fresh parsley, roughly chopped

1 cup (149 g) cherry tomatoes, quartered

½ red onion, thinly sliced

¼ English cucumber, sliced into half-moons

2 ounces (55 g) feta cheese, crumbled

¼ cup (33 g) Kalamata olives, pitted and roughly chopped

2 tablespoons (18 g) capers

FRESH SUMMER QUINOA SALAD

YIELD: SERVES 2

This salad just makes me happy. I don't know why, but it does. This is a classic example of thinking outside the box with salads—not only do I use quinoa as a base, but I also give the salad a sweet twist, with some unconventional ingredients and aromatics. The fruits and veggies are incredibly refreshing and light, and pack a lot of quality nutrients. The sweetness and bite of the honey mustard dressing brings everything together. If you try this, let me know if it makes you happy, too.

INSTRUCTIONS

To make the dressing: In a small jar with a lid, combine all the dressing ingredients. Seal the lid and give the jar a good shake until everything is emulsified and homogenous. Taste it and adjust the sweetness and acidity, if needed.

To make the salad: Cook the quinoa according to the package directions. I cook it in my rice cooker with equal parts water. Let the quinoa cool slightly before assembling the salad.

In a large bowl, combine the cooked quinoa with the remaining salad ingredients. Add your preferred amount of dressing, making sure not to overdress the salad—you can always add more! Toss everything to coat and combine and add more dressing, as needed.

INGREDIENTS FOR DRESSING:

2 tablespoons (30 g) Dijon mustard

2 tablespoons (30 ml) olive oil

1 tablespoon (15 ml) distilled white vinegar

1 tablespoon (15 ml) fresh lemon juice, plus more as needed

1 tablespoon (20 g) honey, plus more as needed

INGREDIENTS FOR SALAD:

¾ cup (138 g) dried quinoa

1 cup (20 g) fresh rocket or arugula

½ apple, diced

¼ English cucumber, diced

Big handful of dried cranberries

Big handful of walnuts, roughly chopped

¼ cup (24 g) fresh mint leaves, finely chopped

CHAPTER 4:

INSTANT CLASSICS

KWOOWK Signatures. These recipes put me on the map and are essential to my cooking life, and so, now, will be to yours!

MEALS THAT GOT ME THROUGH COLLEGE

The Leftover Fried Rice 80

Creamy Dreamy Butter Chicken 83

Leftover Chicken Salad 86

Spicy Cherry Tomato Pasta 89

COMFORT FOODS

My Creamy Veggie-Packed Soup 90

Healthier "Fried" Chicken Wings 92

Easy Chicken Congee 95

Easier Than Fast Food Tacos 96

THE LEFTOVER FRIED RICE

YIELD: SERVES 2

A question I get asked a lot by college students who want to get into cooking is, "What is the first dish I should master?" In my opinion, this leftover fried rice is *the* dish for any beginner home cook. The technique is so versatile that it can create a delicious variety of dishes with inexpensive and readily available ingredients that you wouldn't think to use otherwise. Plus, the beauty of this technique is the customizability. You can include any number of cooked and raw vegetables, leftover proteins, and aromatics.

This version is the one I cook most of the time with what I have in the fridge, but I don't shy away from using other ingredients, like eggplant, leftover cooked broccoli, or even bacon. Another thing I'll note is that I like this fried rice fried. When I cook the rice over high heat, I don't move it around too much, just from time to time, so it can develop little bits of brown crispiness on the bottom.

INGREDIENTS

Vegetable oil for coating the pan

2 large eggs

Kosher salt

½ onion, finely diced

1 scallion, white and green, parts, sliced, divided

½ bell pepper, any color, diced

2 or 3 garlic cloves, thinly sliced

1 cup (140 g) sliced leftover cooked protein (I usually use chicken breast)

3 cups (370 g) cold leftover (day-old) cooked rice

1 teaspoon MSG (optional)

1 cup (130 g) frozen peas

1 tablespoon (15 ml) soy sauce, plus more as needed

1 tablespoon (15 ml) oyster sauce

1 tablespoon (15 ml) rice vinegar, plus more as needed

1½ teaspoons dark soy sauce

1½ teaspoons sesame oil

INSTRUCTIONS

Pro tip: *Fried rice is usually made in a well-seasoned wok over very high heat. I found that it's difficult to get the surface of the wok to heat evenly on a conventional home stovetop, so I think a large nonstick skillet does the job just fine, as you want a lot of cooking surface, and you want that surface to be hot.*

Heat a large nonstick skillet over high heat until it starts smoking. Place a plate or bowl nearby for the cooked eggs. Add enough vegetable oil to coat the skillet and *carefully* spread it around with a paper towel. Reserve the paper towel.

Crack the eggs into a bowl, add a sprinkle of salt, and beat them with a fork to blend. Pour the eggs into the oiled skillet. They

should make a satisfying sizzling noise when hitting the pan. Using a wooden spatula, keep the eggs moving because they will cook quickly. We don't care about the presentation of these eggs; they're going to get completely shredded in the final dish. Transfer the cooked eggs to the plate and wipe out your skillet with the reserved paper towel, adding more oil, if needed.

Add the diced onion, sliced scallion whites (reserve the greens), diced bell pepper, and garlic. Stir-fry for up to 2 minutes until the vegetables soften, making sure not to burn them. Add the protein and stir-fry for 1 minute to give it some browning and infuse it with the aromatics.

Add the cold rice to the skillet, along with a sprinkle of MSG (if using). Use your wooden spatula to break apart big chunks. Don't worry about being too thorough. Stir-fry the rice for 2 to 3 minutes while alternating between moving it around and breaking it apart to letting it cook for

20 to 30 seconds undisturbed to develop some browning. By applying this technique we'll create an evenly distributed texture variation throughout the rice.

Stir in the frozen peas and cook for 1 to 2 minutes. By adding them now, we avoid overcooking them and losing their fresh taste and texture.

Once the peas are cooked, add the soy sauce, oyster sauce, vinegar, dark soy sauce, sesame oil, and cooked egg. Toss until the sauce and egg are evenly distributed throughout the rice.

Turn off the heat and taste the dish. Adjust the seasoning with soy sauce and vinegar to your preference. Finish with the scallion greens scattered on top.

CREAMY DREAMY BUTTER CHICKEN

YIELD: SERVES 2

In my exploration of dishes from around the world, every once in a while, I stumble upon a gem that I can implement in my day-to-day student life, and it completely changes how I view college meals. This is one of those life-altering food discoveries that I've recently made. This is originally an Indian dish, but this is my very nontraditional way of making it that I can rely on for a pretty quick and immensely satisfying meal. The original recipe requires a ton of butter and cream, but I managed to take out most of the fat and still create an amazing dish, which means I can eat more of it and not worry too much about my arteries clogging up. This is delicious served with rice or naan bread, or eaten by itself. Either way, it's going to be one of the best culinary experiences you will create in your home kitchen.

INGREDIENTS FOR MARINADE:

8 ounces (225 g) boneless, skinless chicken breast, cut into bite-size pieces

2 or 3 garlic cloves, minced

1½ tablespoons (23 g) full-fat plain Greek yogurt

2 teaspoons garam masala

1 teaspoon smoked paprika

1 teaspoon garlic powder

1 teaspoon grated peeled fresh ginger

Kosher salt

INGREDIENTS FOR FINISHING:

Olive oil for coating the pan

1½ teaspoons butter

1 yellow onion, sliced

Kosher salt

1 (14-ounce, or 395 g) can crushed tomatoes

1 teaspoon garam masala

1 teaspoon smoked paprika

½ cup (120 ml) low-fat cream

Fresh cilantro for topping

INSTRUCTIONS

To make the marinade: In a large bowl, combine the chicken and all the other marinade ingredients. Season with salt to taste. Using your clean hands, mix everything thoroughly until the marinade evenly coats every piece of chicken. Don't forget to wash your hands after handling raw poultry! Cover the bowl with plastic wrap and marinate in the refrigerator until use, ideally overnight. (Most of the time I just let it sit for 10 minutes or so because I don't have that level of patience.)

To finish the dish: In a large skillet over medium-high heat, heat enough olive oil to coat the pan until it shimmers. Add the marinated chicken. It should make a satisfying sizzling noise when hitting the pan. Cook the chicken on all sides without burning the yogurt too much, about 3 minutes. Focus on browning the chicken, not cooking it through, since we'll do that later. Remove the chicken from the skillet once browned; you should be left with some nice fond (the tasty stuck-on browned bits) on the bottom of the pan.

Turn the heat to medium and add the butter to the hot pan to melt. Add the onion. Sprinkle the onion with salt and let it cook for 2 to 3 minutes, stirring occasionally, until the onion softens.

Stir in the crushed tomatoes and simmer the sauce for about 5 minutes until it thickens. Stir in the garam masala and smoked paprika. Taste the sauce and add more salt, if needed.

Stir in the cream, turn the heat to low, and simmer the sauce for 2 minutes.

Add the chicken to the sauce and gently simmer for 1 to 2 minutes, or until warmed and cooked through. Top the dish with fresh cilantro and serve.

LEFTOVER CHICKEN SALAD

YIELD: SERVES 2

The word "salad" here does not mean a bowl full of leafy greens and a dressing, but, rather, a concoction of cold shredded protein and vegetables bonded together by a creamy substance. I know it doesn't sound amazing, but this is, hands down, my favorite way to use leftover chicken and other common fridge and pantry staples. It is quintessential college cooking done to perfection.

INSTRUCTIONS

Pull the leftover chicken from the fridge (make sure it's cold) and using your clean hands or two forks, shred all the meat into various-size chunks. The meat is easily tearable if you use the grain (see page 19) to your advantage.

In a large bowl, combine the shredded chicken with the scallion, capers, garlic, cranberries, parsley, yogurt, mayonnaise, Dijon, and olive oil.

Using a spoon, whip the ingredients together until everything is well incorporated. I say "whip" because in addition to mixing the ingredient, you want to incorporate a bit of air in the

mixture and slightly emulsify it, meaning to combine the fat and acid by vigorously mixing to create a thick, creamy texture.

Taste and season with salt and pepper.

Fill the buns with a generous amount of chicken salad and top with lettuce and tomato.

Pro tip: *It's all about building layers of complementary flavors and textures using simple ingredients. I use a combination of yogurt, mayo, mustard, and olive oil to provide creaminess and bind the ingredients. Typically, only mayo is used, but my version is not only lower in calories, but also provides a lighter finish and a more complex flavor profile.*

INGREDIENTS

8 ounces (225 g) leftover Straightforward Chicken Breast (page 25; actually any cut will do) or store-bought rotisserie chicken

1 scallion, white and green parts, finely chopped

2 tablespoons (18 g) capers

1 garlic clove, minced

Handful of dried cranberries, roughly chopped

Large handful of chopped fresh parsley

¼ cup (60 g) full-fat plain Greek yogurt

2 tablespoons (30 g) mayonnaise

1 tablespoon (15 g) Dijon mustard

1 tablespoon (15 ml) extra-virgin olive oil

Kosher salt and freshly cracked black pepper

2 burger buns

4 butter lettuce leaves

4 tomato slices, salted

SPICY CHERRY TOMATO PASTA

YIELD: SERVES 2

This is one of the first pasta dishes I learned to make from scratch, and it completely revolutionized my pasta experience. It made me appreciate how much you can make from a few simple ingredients and just a bit of technique, because this dish shines in its simplicity. It packs so much flavor, but it feels subtle at the same time. The cherry tomatoes break down and naturally form a light, creamy sauce, kind of like magic. If you've never made pasta, this should be the first one you try, in my opinion.

INGREDIENTS

Kosher salt

8 ounces (225 g) dried pasta of choice

1 tablespoon (15 ml) extra-virgin olive oil

1 yellow onion, finely diced

2 garlic cloves, crushed

1 fresh red chile, very thinly sliced, seeded for less heat

1 pound (454 g) fresh cherry tomatoes

½ cup (20 g) coarsely chopped fresh basil

Grated parmesan cheese for serving (optional)

INSTRUCTIONS

Cook the pasta in a large pot of salted water according to the package directions until al dente. Reserve about 1 cup (240 ml) of the pasta cooking water, then drain the pasta.

In a large saucepan over medium heat, heat the olive oil until it shimmers. Add the onion, garlic, and chile. Cook the aromatics for 4 to 5 minutes, stirring occasionally, until they become soft and fragrant.

Add the whole cherry tomatoes, generously season with about 2 big pinches of salt, and give them a toss in the pan. Add a splash of water and cover the pan with a lid. Now, get ready for the magic to happen: As the cherry tomatoes cook, they will start bursting and releasing their juices that will naturally form a sauce. This process should take 6 to 10 minutes, during which you should stir the tomatoes every couple of minutes.

Add a splash of pasta water to complete the sauce, adding more, in small amounts, if the sauce is too thick. Sprinkle with fresh basil to finish, then add the cooked pasta and toss to coat and combine.

Optionally, top the pasta with some grated parmesan cheese, but I prefer it sans parm.

MY CREAMY VEGGIE-PACKED SOUP

YIELD: SERVES 4

A good soup is hard to beat. It provides warmth, comfort, and a feeling of home. This is surely the case with this recipe. Just the smell of the vegetables cooking in butter, getting slightly browned, instantly transports me to my childhood. This simple recipe does require a bit of vegetable chopping. Don't be too precise, though, because it's all gonna get blended up anyway.

INGREDIENTS

2 tablespoons (28 g) butter

1 yellow onion, diced

3 garlic cloves, peeled

2 medium-size carrots, diced

2 parsnips, peeled and diced

2 or 3 medium-size potatoes, diced

2 celery stalks, diced

Kosher salt and ground black pepper

8 cups (1.9 L) Veggie Stock from Scraps (page 23), or store-bought, plus more as needed

2 cups (260 g) frozen peas

Heavy cream for topping (optional)

Finely minced fresh parsley for topping

Sliced bread or naan for serving

INSTRUCTIONS

In a Dutch oven over medium heat, melt the butter. Add the diced onion and garlic cloves. Sweat the onion for 2 to 3 minutes until it softens and becomes fragrant, stirring occasionally.

Add the carrots, parsnips, potatoes, and celery. Generously season the vegetables with salt and cook for 5 to 6 minutes, stirring and turning them every 30 seconds or so. The goal is to get some slight browning and kick-start the cooking process, as well as making sure the flavors get to know each other. You'll smell that earthy, buttery aroma, and that's a good sign.

Pour in enough veggie stock to completely cover the vegetables. Bring to a simmer and turn the heat to low. Simmer the vegetables in the stock for 20 to 25 minutes until they are soft and tender.

Using a hand blender, or carefully transferring everything to a regular blender, blend the soup until smooth, creamy, and thick. Return the soup to the pot, if needed.

Turn off the heat. Add the frozen peas and let them cook in the residual heat for a few minutes. Taste the soup and season with salt and pepper.

To serve, I top the soup with a swirl of cream, some fresh parsley, and a drizzle of olive oil. I also like some hot naan bread with this soup, but you do you.

Refrigerate leftovers in an airtight container for 3 to 4 days.

HEALTHIER "FRIED" CHICKEN WINGS

YIELD: SERVES 2

Okay, this is technically not fried chicken—it's baked—but stay with me. I've been looking for a way to get the experience of fried chicken without the calories for the longest time because it's one of my favorite comfort foods. Turns out, most of the calories comes from the fat used for deep-frying. Now, the challenge is getting the same level of crispiness and satisfaction from an oven-baked wing. With this simple combination of ingredients and a few tricks, I was able to find an easy, mess-free way to create a finger-licking chicken wing experience. The combination of flour, cornstarch, baking powder, and salt in the coating works toward getting the crispiest exterior possible.

The recipe might sound overly simple—it doesn't have a buttermilk marinade or a multi-station breading process—but, to me, the results this convenient recipe yields make this comfort meal achievable even during the busiest days. While the wings bake, I often make a simple yogurt dip (see Herby Yogurt Sauce and Dip, page 26) and, sometimes, a fresh tomato salad to have on the side.

INGREDIENTS

2 pounds (908 g) chicken wings

1 tablespoon (7.5 g) all-purpose flour

1 tablespoon (8 g) cornstarch

2 teaspoons baking powder

2 teaspoons kosher salt

2 teaspoons ground white pepper

2 teaspoons smoked paprika

2 teaspoons dried thyme

2 teaspoons garlic powder

2 teaspoons onion powder

1 teaspoon ground ginger

1 teaspoon ground mustard (optional)

½ teaspoon cayenne pepper

INSTRUCTIONS

Place the chicken wings on a clean baking sheet or other flat work surface and pat dry using paper towels. It's important to remove as much moisture as you can because this correlates directly to the crispiness of the final product. The drier, the better. Place the dried chicken wings in a large bowl.

In a small bowl, stir together the flour, cornstarch, baking powder, and all the spices until evenly combined. Sprinkle the seasoned flour over the wings, spreading it as evenly as possible. Using your clean hands, distribute the coating until every piece of chicken is covered evenly.

One by one, remove the chicken wings and gently shake off any excess seasoning, then place them on a wire rack set over a clean baking sheet, spacing the wings so they don't touch.

Pro tip: *The wire rack allows for more air circulation around the wings while cooking, which leads to more even cooking and, you guessed it, more crispiness.*

Optionally, but recommended, chill the coated wings in the refrigerator for at least 2 hours, uncovered, to allow the baking powder and salt to interact with the chicken skin. Place the chicken toward the bottom of the fridge so raw chicken juices do not drip off, potentially contaminating your food. You may be tempted to pass on

this step (and if you do, the wings will still be delicious), but if you have time on your hands, it makes a difference in the results. Preheat the oven to 350°F (180°C, or gas mark 4).

After chilling (or not), bake the chicken wings for 25 minutes. Flip the wings and bake for 10 minutes more, or longer, until evenly cooked on all sides. Observe the color and texture of the skin: You're looking for a golden-brown color and a crispy but not dry exterior.

EASY CHICKEN CONGEE

YIELD: SERVES 2

I discovered this dish during my "Rating Breakfast Around the World" series. It is a rice porridge traditionally served for breakfast in many areas of China, and it's one of the most comforting dishes I've ever made. And, not only is it satisfying and heart-warming, but it's also affordable. Rice is an inexpensive ingredient, and you need only a small amount for a lot of porridge. This recipe also uses an interesting technique of cooking the chicken in the residual heat of the porridge, which produces incredibly tender chicken.

INSTRUCTIONS

To make the marinade: Cut the chicken into bite-size pieces, as thin as you can to cook more easily in the rice. Place the chicken in a medium-size bowl and add all the marinade ingredients. Using your clean hands, mix everything to coat the chicken fully with marinade. Cover the bowl with plastic wrap and refrigerate until use.

To make the porridge: In a large pot over high heat, bring the water to a boil. Add the bouillon cube and boil until it dissolves completely. Turn the heat to medium and add the rinsed rice. Give it a stir, then partially cover the pot and simmer for 25 minutes. The rice should begin to resemble oatmeal in consistency. The individual grains should start to break down, and the starch from the rice will thicken the water.

Add the ginger and scallion to flavor the porridge, and taste the congee; add salt as needed. Re-cover the pot partially and cook for 10 minutes, or until the porridge becomes thick and homogenous.

Add the chicken to the boiling rice while stirring, making sure the pieces are separated. Cook for 4 to 5 minutes, or until there are no raw, pink spots left in the chicken. Turn off the heat and serve the congee in a bowl topped with cilantro.

INGREDIENTS FOR CHICKEN AND MARINADE:

6 ounces (170 g) boneless, skinless chicken thighs or breast (I prefer thighs)

1 teaspoon cornstarch

1 teaspoon soy sauce

1 teaspoon dark soy sauce

1 teaspoon sesame oil

1 garlic clove, minced

INGREDIENTS FOR RICE:

3 to 5 cups (720 ml to 1.2 L) water (depending on your thickness preference; I always use 4)

1 chicken bouillon cube

½ cup (100 g) raw white rice, rinsed

3 or 4 thin slices peeled fresh ginger, cut into thin matchsticks

1 scallion, white and green parts, sliced

Kosher salt

Fresh cilantro for topping

FASTER THAN FAST FOOD TACOS

YIELD: SERVES 2

Taco night is a weekly occurrence in my house, and one of our favorite activities. We love the idea of having lots of different ingredients to choose from laid out on the table. The act of building your own taco, building flavors and textures, is such a fun culinary experience, especially with a loved one. What's great is that with just a tiny bit of effort you can create your own taco experience—faster than delivery and infinitely better quality. And by the way, we eat about four tacos each, so adjust the quantity based on your preference.

INSTRUCTIONS

Warm the tortillas: Place a large skillet over high heat and, one at a time, heat the tortillas for 10 to 15 seconds per side until they develop some charred spots. Set aside, wrapped in a clean kitchen towel.

To make the beef: Turn the heat under the skillet to medium-high. Pour in a swirl of olive oil to coat the skillet. Add the onion and garlic and sweat the vegetables for 1 to 2 minutes, stirring constantly. Add the ground beef and break it apart using the back of a wooden spoon. Add all the seasonings to the beef and season to taste with salt. Give the beef a few stirs until the spices are incorporated. Cook the beef for 7 to 8 minutes, stirring occasionally, until it's fully browned and cooked through. Cover the skillet, turn the heat to the lowest setting, and keep the beef warm until use.

To make the guacamole: In a medium-size glass bowl, combine the avocado, lime juice, tomato, garlic, and salt to taste. Using a fork, roughly mash the avocado and tomato. Don't worry about being too thorough; some chunkiness is highly advised.

Arrange all your ingredients, including toppings, on a table, along with your favorite hot sauces. You can combine these ingredients however you want. I add some ground beef first, a drizzle of hot sauce on top of it, a layer of guacamole, some kidney beans, sour cream, fresh cilantro, and finally some pickled onions. That's right, I don't do lettuce on my tacos, but you can.

INGREDIENTS

8 small (8-inch, or 20 cm) flour tortillas

INGREDIENTS FOR BEEF:

Olive oil for coating the pan

½ white onion, finely diced

2 or 3 garlic cloves, minced

1 pound (454 g) ground beef

2 teaspoons smoked paprika

2 teaspoons ground cumin

1 teaspoon garlic powder

1 teaspoon onion powder

Kosher salt

INGREDIENTS FOR GUACAMOLE:

2 ripe avocados, pitted and diced

Juice of ½ lime

1 or 2 Roma tomatoes, finely diced

1 garlic clove, minced

Kosher salt

INGREDIENTS FOR OTHER TOPPINGS:

Sour cream

Shredded lettuce

Canned red kidney beans, drained and rinsed

Pickled red onions (see Pickled Red Onions and Other Things, page 24) for topping

Fresh cilantro

Hot sauce

CHAPTER 5:

DINNERTIME

Sometimes, it's nice to slow down and enjoy life a little. A home-cooked dinner is my way of doing that. You should try it, too.

DINNER FOR ONE

The Best Black Bean Burger
You'll Ever Eat   100

The Ultimate Chicken and
Broccoli Stir-Fry   103

Instant Ramen Upgrade   106

DATE NIGHT RECIPES

Homemade Gnocchi with
Peas and Walnuts   108

Aglio e Olio e Cacio
e Pepe   112

Sweet and Spicy Tofu
Noodles   114

Roasted Veggie Risotto   117

THE BEST BLACK BEAN BURGER YOU'LL EVER EAT

YIELD: SERVES 1

The first time I made this I was so surprised by how good it was, I legitimately considered never eating a regular burger again. Of course, then I realized I have enough love for both regular burgers and black bean burgers in my heart. Don't expect a beef burger experience from this. Go into it like a new dish, then you'll understand just how good it is. The bean patty provides crispiness on the outside and a hearty and satisfying inside, rich in fiber and other important nutrients, and it complements the simple fresh toppings. Beans are a cheap and nutrient-rich food that everyone should eat more of, and making it into a burger like this might just be one of the best ways to eat beans. This recipe easily doubles, triples, or more to feed a crowd.

INGREDIENTS FOR PATTY:

½ (14-ounce, 395 g) can black beans, drained and rinsed under cold water

1 large egg

½ shallot, finely diced

2 garlic cloves, minced

1 teaspoon smoked paprika

1 teaspoon ground cumin

1 teaspoon dried thyme

1 to 2 tablespoons (7 to 14 g) bread crumbs

2 ounces (55 g) feta cheese, crumbled

Flaky sea salt

1 tablespoon (15 ml) neutral oil

INGREDIENTS FOR SAUCE:

1 tablespoon (15 g) full-fat plain Greek yogurt

1 teaspoon chili oil, plus more as needed

INGREDIENTS FOR FINISHING:

1 teaspoon butter

1 burger bun

1 medium-size tomato

Kosher salt

Small handful of arugula

Pickled red onions (see Pickled Red Onions and Other Things, page 24) for topping

INSTRUCTIONS

Preheat the oven to 350°F (180°C, or gas mark 4). Line a baking sheet with parchment paper.

To make the patty: Spread the beans on the prepared baking sheet and bake for 20 minutes. We need to dry the beans to make sure our patty doesn't turn mushy.

In the meantime, make an easy sauce: In a small bowl, stir together the yogurt and chili oil. Taste and adjust the chili oil, if needed.

While the beans bake, prep the other ingredients, too: Melt the butter in a skillet over medium heat and toast the buns until golden brown; cut 2 or 3 slices from the tomato and season the slices with salt.

To finish the patty: Transfer the beans to a large bowl and roughly mash them using a fork. The reason we're using a fork is because we want some textural variety, and not a silky-smooth mashed product. Add the egg to the smashed beans and beat it in with the fork. Stir in the shallot, garlic, and all the seasonings. Stir in 1 tablespoon (7 g) of bread crumbs and adjust the amount based on the consistency (no two burgers are alike). Look for an easily moldable mixture that holds its shape. Finally, mix in the feta.

Shape your mixture into 1 or 2 tennis ball–size portions. If you get two patties, save one for later, or double stack your burgers. Using your clean hands, shape them into ¾-inch (2 cm)-thick patties. Lightly season the patties with flaky salt on both sides.

In a skillet over medium-high heat, heat the oil until it shimmers. Add the patties and cook for about 2 minutes per side until browned, carefully flipping the patties with a spatula.

To assemble, spread half the sauce over the bottom bun. Top with arugula, tomato slices, and then your bean patty. Spread the remaining yogurt sauce on the patty, and finish with some pickled onions. Top with the remaining bun.

THE ULTIMATE CHICKEN AND BROCCOLI STIR-FRY

YIELD: SERVES 1

The stir-fry is one of the most essential dishes for a home cook to master, because the technique behind it allows you endless variations that you'll never get bored of. This dish is one of my favorite ways to sneak more veggies into my life. I load it up with as much broccoli as I can and add bell peppers, scallions, and, sometimes, even asparagus. Chicken and broccoli is commonly regarded as a tasteless bodybuilder "healthy" meal, but we can take most of those nutritional benefits and create an amazingly delicious dish on top of that. Serve with rice or noodles, or eat it by itself. Either way, get ready to make this a lot more frequently.

INGREDIENTS FOR MARINATED CHICKEN:

1 boneless, skinless chicken breast, cut into bite-size pieces

1 tablespoon (15 ml) soy sauce

1 tablespoon (15 ml) rice vinegar

1½ teaspoons dark soy sauce

1 teaspoon sesame oil

2 teaspoons cornstarch

INGREDIENTS FOR SAUCE:

1 tablespoon (15 ml) soy sauce

1 tablespoon (15 ml) oyster sauce

1½ teaspoons dark soy sauce

2 teaspoons cornstarch

¼ cup (60 ml) water

INGREDIENTS FOR VEGETABLES AND AROMATICS:

Vegetable oil for frying

1 cup (71 g) broccoli florets, chopped into bite-size pieces

½ bell pepper, any color, sliced into matchsticks

Kosher salt

1 scallion, white and green parts, roughly chopped

2 garlic cloves, sliced

1 tablespoon (6 g) minced peeled fresh ginger

½ fresh red chile, sliced, seeded for less heat

INGREDIENTS FOR GARNISH:

1 tablespoon (8 g) sesame seeds

1 scallion, white and green parts, finely sliced

INSTRUCTIONS

To make the marinated chicken: In a large bowl, combine the chicken and all the other ingredients for the marinade. Using your clean hands, mix and distribute the ingredients evenly, making sure all the chicken is well coated. Set the chicken aside for at least 15 minutes to marinate, which is just enough time to prep the other ingredients.

To make the sauce: In a small bowl, whisk the soy sauce, oyster sauce, dark soy sauce, cornstarch, and water until blended. The cornstarch will provide the signature thick, glossy finish to the dish. Set aside.

To cook the chicken: Heat a large pan, skillet, or wok over high heat until it just starts to smoke. Pour in about 1 tablespoon (15 ml) of oil to coat the pan. Add the chicken to the hot pan and stir-fry for 3 to 4 minutes until all the pieces are cooked through and no longer pink. Transfer the chicken to a plate.

To incorporate the vegetables and aromatics: Add the broccoli and bell pepper to the hot pan. Season with a bit of salt and cook for 1 minute, tossing and stirring. Add a splash of water to the pan and cover it with a lid. Cook for about 5 minutes, covered, stirring the vegetables every couple of minutes. We're looking to cook the veggies fast: We don't want to cook them to a mush, just enough so they lose that raw edge and soften a bit. Transfer the veggies to another plate, just like the chicken.

Add a swirl of oil to the pan, and add the aromatics—scallion, garlic, ginger, and red chile—all at once. Stir-fry for 2 minutes, making sure not to burn them.

Pour in the sauce we made earlier and cook for 2 to 3 minutes, stirring constantly, until it reduces and thickens.

Return the chicken and veggies to the pan. Reduce the heat to medium and cook, tossing everything together, until the sauce evenly coats the ingredients.

Finish with a sprinkle of sesame seeds and finely sliced scallion.

INSTANT RAMEN UPGRADE

YIELD: SERVES 1

Instant ramen noodles, the stereotypical cheap meal for students, have a bad rep because they're one-dimensional, unexciting , and not very nutritious. I have a lot of respect for instant ramen, and appreciate the nostalgic, simple experience it provides, but I'm here to elevate that experience on all fronts. I want an instant noodle dish that is more nutritious, tastes better, and makes you feel as though you're dining at a restaurant, all with very little effort.

INGREDIENTS FOR SAUCE:

1 tablespoon (15 ml) soy sauce

1 tablespoon (15 ml) oyster sauce

1½ teaspoons dark soy sauce

1 teaspoon rice vinegar

1 teaspoon cornstarch

3 tablespoons (45 ml) water

INGREDIENTS FOR RAMEN:

1 (3-ounce, or 85 g) package instant ramen noodles (seasoning packet discarded)

1 tablespoon (15 ml) neutral oil

2 garlic cloves, minced

1 fresh red chile, sliced, seeded for less heat

2 scallions, 1 sliced on the diagonal and 1, green part only, very thinly sliced, separated

1 teaspoon minced peeled fresh ginger

½ cup (35 g) sliced shiitake mushrooms

½ cup (65 g) frozen green peas

1 large soft-boiled egg (see Boiled Eggs, the Easy Way, page 22)

1 teaspoon sesame oil

Fresh cilantro for topping

INSTRUCTIONS

To make the sauce: In a small bowl, stir together all the sauce ingredients until blended. The cornstarch will provide the signature thick, glossy finish to the dish. Set aside.

To make the ramen: Cook the ramen noodles according to the package directions. Drain and rinse under cold water. Set aside.

In a wok or large skillet over medium-high heat, heat 1 tablespoon (15 ml) of oil until it starts to smoke. Add the garlic, chile, 1 scallion (white and green parts), and ginger. Cook the aromatics for 2 minutes, stirring constantly, until fragrant.

Add the mushrooms. Stir-fry for 2 minutes. Focus on getting some browning and cooking them fast; we don't want to steam them in their own water. If needed, turn the heat to high. Add the frozen peas. Cook for 1 minute.

Pour the sauce into the pan and cook for 2 to 3 minutes until it reduces and thickens only slightly, preserving its thinness to interact better with the noodles.

Add the cooked noodles to the skillet and turn the heat to medium. Toss the noodles to coat them with the sauce. Turn off the heat and top with the egg (if using), drizzle on the sesame oil, and garnish with the scallion greens and cilantro.

HOMEMADE GNOCCHI WITH PEAS AND WALNUTS

YIELD: SERVES 2

If you're familiar with gnocchi (and how to pronounce it correctly: NYOH-kee), then you know its luxurious, pillowy texture is enough to enhance any date and most certainly impress your crush, especially when you tell them you made it yourself. Gnocchi is really not complicated to make; it just requires a few simple steps and a bit of patience, and a few other simple but powerful ingredients to shine. This is my twist on the classic brown butter sage gnocchi. A special treat for sure.

INGREDIENTS FOR GNOCCHI:

2 leftover baked russet potatoes

1 large egg, whisked

1 cup (120 g) all-purpose flour, plus more for dusting and as needed

1 teaspoon kosher salt

INGREDIENTS FOR BROWN BUTTER SAGE SAUCE:

2 tablespoons (28 g) butter

10 to 12 fresh sage leaves

½ cup (64 g) frozen peas

1 small bunch fresh parsley, roughly chopped

½ cup (50 g) walnuts, finely chopped

Grated zest of ½ lemon

Grated parmesan cheese for topping

Flaky sea salt and freshly cracked black pepper

INSTRUCTIONS

Pro tip: *If you have no leftover baked potatoes handy, bake some fresh. Pierce 2 potatoes with a fork on all sides and bake in a 400°F (200°C, or gas mark 6) oven for 45 to 50 minutes until they pierce easily with a fork.*

To make the gnocchi: Peel off and discard the skin from the baked potatoes. Place the potatoes in a medium-size bowl and, using a fork or a potato ricer, mash to a fine, fluffy consistency.

Add the whisked egg and mix that in until fully incorporated. Sift in the flour and add the salt. Use your clean hands to incorporate the flour into the potato mixture. You should get an easily manageable dough you can knead.

Lightly dust a clean work surface with flour and place the dough out on it. Knead the dough for about 3 minutes until smooth: Alternate between a folding and pushing motion on all sides. Get a little rough with it; I slap the dough gently on my counter between folds. If the dough is too sticky, add a small amount of flour and knead it in.

Divide the dough into 4 sections and roll them out with your hand into 15- to 20-inch (38 to 50 cm)-long ropes. Using a sharp knife, cut the dough into ¾-inch (2 cm) pieces.

Using a well-floured index finger, gently poke some holes into the gnocchi. The holes will act as pockets to catch the sauce. Lightly dust the gnocchi with flour and reserve until use. You can also refrigerate the gnocchi, lightly dusted with flour, in a zip-top bag and finish the dish the next day.

To finish the gnocchi and make the sauce: Bring a large pot of generously salted water to a boil over high heat. Gently add the gnocchi and cook until they naturally float to the top. Using a spider, gently fish them out of the water and place them in a bowl. Don't throw out the cooking water; we will need some later.

In a medium-size saucepan or skillet over medium heat, melt the butter and let it cook until it's bubbling. Add the sage leaves. Let these cook, virtually undisturbed, for 4 to 5 minutes, occasionally swirling the butter around and flipping the sage leaves, if needed. The goal is to brown the butter and crisp the sage. Remember, browning is not burning, so watch the heat.

Once the butter has a dark golden-brown color, add the gnocchi and make sure every piece (or most pieces) touches the pan. Cook the gnocchi in the brown butter for 4 to 6 minutes until it develops a golden-brown crispy bottom, then flip them.

Add about ¼ cup (60 ml) of the reserved pasta water and toss the gnocchi with the brown butter until a thicker sauce forms. Turn the heat to low and add the frozen peas, parsley, walnuts, lemon zest, parmesan, salt to taste, and a generous amount of pepper. Toss everything until the ingredients are evenly distributed and the peas are cooked, about 2 minutes.

Top with more grated parmesan to serve, if you're feeling adventurous, and get ready for your date to be impressed.

AGLIO E OLIO E CACIO E PEPE

YIELD: SERVES 2

I am stepping into dangerous territory, messing with two traditional Italian dishes like aglio e olio (pasta with garlic and olive oil) and cacio e pepe (pasta with cheese and pepper)—hide your Italian grandmas! But honestly, I don't really care, because I like it this way, and it also makes a fun-sounding name. We will, essentially, take the simple core ingredients that make up these two famously simple pasta dishes and mash them together in a cheesy, garlicky, peppery, tasty way. I do suggest, however, that you invest a bit in a higher-quality pasta, as it makes a pretty big difference in the results. This dish does take a bit of technique and requires a sense of timing, but I believe anyone can master it with practice.

INGREDIENTS

6 ounces (170 g) high-quality dried spaghetti

3 tablespoons (45 ml) extra-virgin olive oil

1 tablespoon (8.5 g) whole peppercorns

2 garlic cloves, finely sliced

1 fresh red chile, sliced, seeded for less heat

1 cup (60 g) freshly grated pecorino Romano cheese

1 big bunch fresh parsley, roughly chopped

Freshly ground black pepper (optional)

INSTRUCTIONS

First, bring a medium-size pot or skillet of generously salted water to a boil over high heat. Drop in the spaghetti and cook for about 8 minutes, checking after 5, until just below al dente.

Pro tip: *We want to use just enough water to cover the pasta: By minimizing the amount of water, we maximize the amount of starch, which helps create a glossy, thick sauce.*

At the same time you drop in the pasta, in another skillet over medium heat, heat the olive oil. Grind the peppercorns to a course powder using a mortar and pestle or a peppermill and add them to the hot oil. Add the garlic and chile as well, and gently cook them in the oil for 3 to 4 minutes. We don't want an aggressive fry, so if it gets too bubbly around the garlic and you're afraid it might burn, immediately turn the heat to low. Keep this mixture moving, adjusting the heat to low, if needed, until the pasta has cooked to just below al dente (it will finish in the skillet).

Once the pasta is ready, turn the heat under the skillet with the oil to medium. Carefully add a ladleful of pasta cooking water to the oil. Using tongs, pull the almost-cooked spaghetti from the water and add it to the oil. Sprinkle the cheese on top and begin tossing and stirring vigorously. The goal here is to get a thickened, emulsified sauce, without any lumps of cheese. Add a few more ladlefuls of pasta water and cook, reducing the sauce, until the pasta is al dente, 2 to 3 minutes total.

At this point, assess the thickness of your sauce. Is it too dry? Add a bit more pasta water and toss until thickened. Is it too thin? Simply cook it for a bit longer, tossing and stirring constantly.

Pro tip: *Always go for a bit of a thinner sauce because by the time you plate it and it sits for a couple of minutes, the sauce will be the perfect consistency.*

Add the fresh parsley and toss it with the pasta. Now, you're ready to plate. I finish with some freshly ground black pepper, just to get an extra kick, but you do you. Sorry, Italians!

SWEET AND SPICY TOFU NOODLES

YIELD: SERVES 2

Noodles for a date? Sign me up. This amazing vegetarian dish is rich in sweet, garlicky, and umami flavors, and packs a spicy kick, too. The glossy sauce coats crispy, pillowy tofu bites, all delivered by a light but satisfying base of rice noodles.

INSTRUCTIONS

To make the sauce: In a small bowl, stir together all the sauce ingredients until blended. Set aside.

To make the tofu and noodles: Cook the rice noodles according to the package directions. Drain and rinse the noodles thoroughly under cold water to make sure they don't stick together. Set aside.

In a medium-size bowl, combine the tofu, salt, and cornstarch. Using your clean hands, toss the tofu until every piece is coated on all sides. This will help crisp the tofu as it cooks.

In a large skillet or wok over medium-high heat, heat the oil until it shimmers, swirling to coat the bottom of the skillet.

Add the tofu, making sure the pan isn't too crowded so every piece touches the skillet's surface. Cook for 3 to 4 minutes, undisturbed, until golden brown. Carefully flip each piece and repeat on the other side. Transfer the tofu to a plate.

In the skillet, still over medium-high heat, combine the chiles, onion, garlic, and half the scallions. Add a bit more oil if the skillet seems dry. Stir-fry for about 2 minutes until fragrant, then pour in the sauce. Cook for 1 minute to reduce the sauce, then add the tofu and noodles. Toss everything until the noodles and tofu are fully coated. Add some water if things are too thick.

Finish with a drizzle of sesame oil, a sprinkle of sesame seeds, and the remaining scallions.

INGREDIENTS FOR SAUCE:

2 tablespoons (30 ml) soy sauce

2 tablespoons (40 g) honey

1 tablespoon (15 ml) rice vinegar

2 teaspoons cornstarch

1 tablespoon (15 ml) water

INGREDIENTS FOR TOFU AND NOODLES:

4 ounces (115 g) dried rice noodles

½ pound (227 g) extra-firm tofu, chopped into bite-size cubes

1 teaspoon kosher salt

2 tablespoons (16 g) cornstarch

2 tablespoons (30 ml) vegetable oil, plus more as needed

2 fresh red chiles, sliced, seeded for less heat

½ red onion, finely diced

4 garlic cloves, minced

2 scallions, white and green parts, sliced on the diagonal

Toasted sesame oil for garnish

Sesame seeds for garnish

ROASTED VEGGIE RISOTTO

YIELD: SERVES 2

In my experience, making good risotto is all about a little technique and some patience. Sneaking in a lot of vegetables elevates its taste and nutritional value. That's what this roasted veggie risotto is all about.

INSTRUCTIONS

Preheat the oven to 350°F (180°C, or gas mark 4). Line a baking sheet with parchment paper.

To make the sauce: Place the tomatoes, bell peppers, eggplant, and garlic on the prepared baking sheet. Generously drizzle with olive oil and season with salt. Bake for 30 to 35 minutes until the vegetables are soft. Transfer the veggies to a large bowl and blend with an immersion blender, or mash with a potato masher until smooth. Set aside.

To make the risotto: In a small saucepan over medium heat, warm the broth.

In a medium-size saucepan over medium heat, heat the olive oil until it shimmers. Add the onion and sauté for 2 minutes until it begins to soften and become fragrant, stirring constantly.

Add the rice and stir to combine with the onion and coat with the oil. Pour in the wine to deglaze the pan, stirring to scrape up any browned bits from the bottom. Let reduce for 1 minute, stirring, until a thick sauce forms.

Pour 1 cup (240 ml) of the hot broth into the rice. Using a wooden spoon or rubber spatula, cook, stirring constantly, until most of the stock is absorbed by the rice. Gradually add more stock, about ½ cup (120 ml) at a time, cooking and stirring constantly until it is absorbed before adding more, until the rice is cooked to al dente. You may not use all the broth.

When the rice is al dente and has a creamy consistency, stir in the roasted veggies. Add thyme leaves to taste and serve, topped with a glorious mound of parmesan.

INGREDIENTS FOR SAUCE:

10 ounces (280 g) cherry tomatoes

2 red bell peppers, sliced

1 eggplant, diced

3 garlic cloves, peeled

Olive oil for coating the vegetables

Kosher salt

INGREDIENTS FOR RISOTTO:

4 cups (960 ml) vegetable broth

1 tablespoon (15 ml) olive oil

½ red onion, finely diced

¾ cup (144 g) raw risotto (arborio) rice

Splash of white wine

Fresh thyme leaves for seasoning

Grated parmesan cheese for garnish

CHAPTER 6:

PASTA AND BOWL FOOD

There's something equally comforting and efficient about eating a nutritious, warm, cooked meal from a bowl—multiple ingredients, colors, textures, all coming together in one bowl you can eat on the couch. The bowl format also allows for creativity and fun, which are, ultimately, as important as anything when it comes to cooking and eating in my world.

PASTA

Herby Homemade Pesto
Pasta with Tomatoes   120

Chicken Fajita Pasta   123

Creamy Mushroom Pasta   124

One-Pot Chicken and
Broccoli Pasta   126

BOWL FOOD

Cheap Chicken Poke Bowl 128

Epic Tofu Burrito Bowl   131

Loaded Veggie Quinoa
Bowl   135

Creamy Chickpea Curry   136

HERBY HOMEMADE PESTO PASTA WITH TOMATOES

YIELD: SERVES 2

Garlicky, herby, goodness. These are the first three words that come to mind when I think of pesto. This classic sauce is deserving of its spot as one of the most popular and loved pasta sauces ever. When I make pesto, I keep it simple. Just throw the ingredients in a food processor, and let it do the work, while I help it along with some olive oil. After that, I refrigerate my pesto, where it will keep for up to four days, and use it for multiple things (I sometimes even just spread it on bread with some tomatoes). Homemade pesto is so much better than store-bought. For this simple dish, I just add some pasta and pasta water and boom: a pasta sauce is born.

INSTRUCTIONS

To make the pesto: In a food processor, combine all the pesto ingredients with 6 tablespoons (90 ml) of olive oil. Blend until thoroughly mixed and a paste forms. If, during the blending process, you feel the pesto is too thick, add up to 2 tablespoons (30 ml) more olive oil to loosen things up. Keep in mind, we're not looking for a smooth, velvety sauce here; we will make that once we make the pasta. Refrigerate the pesto in a sealed container for up to 4 days.

To make the pasta: Cook the spaghetti in a large pot of salted water according to the package directions until al dente. I do this next to the skillet I make my sauce in and add the pasta to the water the moment I start working on the sauce. The pasta cook time is pretty much the same as the sauce, so I can just transfer the pasta to the sauce skillet.

Start the sauce: In a large skillet over medium heat, heat the olive oil until it shimmers. Add the cherry tomato halves and sprinkle with a generous pinch of salt and the red pepper flakes. Give the tomatoes a toss to coat with the oil and seasoning, and cover the skillet with a lid. Cook for 6 to 8 minutes, stirring occasionally, until the tomatoes soften.

Add 3 to 4 generous spoonfuls of pesto to the tomatoes, as well as a generous ladleful of the pasta cooking water. The starchy water will help form the sauce. Turn the heat under the skillet to medium-low. Once the pasta is done, use tongs to transfer it to the sauce without shaking off the excess liquid (we need all that starch). Toss the pasta with the sauce until it's well coated.

Now, it's time to adjust. Not salty enough? Add some salt. Not pesto-y enough? (Is that a word?) Add some pesto. Too thick and not saucy enough? Add some pasta water. Is it too watery? Cook for a bit more.

By the end, you'll have an amazing pesto pasta dish you can top with any amount of grated parmesan cheese you want and, very important, some chopped nuts for a little texture.

INGREDIENTS FOR PESTO:

2 cups (70 g) fresh basil leaves

1 bunch fresh parsley

2 tablespoons (16 g) chopped cashews or walnuts (or pine nuts, if it fits your budget)

2 or 3 garlic cloves, roughly chopped

¼ cup (25 g) grated parmesan cheese

Grated zest of ½ lemon (optional, but highly recommended)

Kosher salt

6 to 8 tablespoons (90 to 120 ml) extra-virgin olive oil (invest in higher quality here)

INGREDIENTS FOR PASTA:

Kosher salt

4 ounces (115 g) dried spaghetti

1 tablespoon (15 ml) olive oil

10 ounces (280 g) cherry tomatoes, halved

1½ teaspoons red pepper flakes

Grated parmesan cheese for garnish

Chopped nuts (whatever you used in the pesto) for garnish

CHICKEN FAJITA PASTA

YIELD: SERVES 2

I eat this chicken and melty cheesy pasta when I want to treat myself with a hefty bowl of goodness. I wouldn't exactly call this a weight-loss meal, but I did pack quite a bit of veggies and protein into it, leading to a nutritionally complex serving.

INSTRUCTIONS

Cook the pasta in a large pot of water according to the package directions until al dente. Reserve ½ cup (120 ml) of the cooking water. Drain and rinse the pasta.

In a medium-size bowl, combine the chicken and fajita seasoning. Use tongs to coat the chicken with the seasoning.

In a large skillet over medium heat, heat the olive oil until it shimmers. Add the coated chicken and cook for 4 to 5 minutes, turning to cook all sides, or until fully cooked and no longer pink. Transfer the chicken to a plate.

In the same skillet still over medium heat, with the nice chicken fond on the bottom, add just a bit more oil if things look dry, then add the onion, red and green bell peppers, and a generous pinch of salt. Cover the skillet with a lid and cook for 6 to 7 minutes until the vegetables soften, stirring occasionally to avoid burning.

Pour in the wine to deglaze the pan, scraping up the browned bits from the bottom. Stir in the tomato paste thoroughly, then the cream. Turn the heat to medium-low. Simmer for 1 to 2 minutes until the sauce thickens slightly.

Add the cooked pasta to the sauce, along with the cheese (if using). Toss and stir the pasta with the sauce. Add the reserved pasta water if the sauce needs to loosen up. You should have a creamy, cheesy, stretchy pasta. Finish with pepper to taste.

INGREDIENTS

4 ounces (115 g) dried long pasta (spaghetti, linguine, bucatini)

2 boneless, skinless chicken breasts, chopped into bite-size pieces

1 (1.25-ounce, or 35 g) packet fajita seasoning mix

1 tablespoon (15 ml) olive oil, plus more as needed

1 white onion, sliced

½ red bell pepper, sliced

½ green bell pepper, sliced

Kosher salt

Generous splash of white wine, chicken broth, or water

2 tablespoons (32 g) tomato paste

1 cup (240 ml) heavy cream or low-fat cream (if you want fewer calories)

Big handful of shredded pepper Jack cheese (optional, but highly recommended)

Freshly cracked black pepper

CREAMY MUSHROOM PASTA

YIELD: SERVES 2

Can we take a moment and acknowledge the awesomeness of mushrooms? They're packed with nutrients, sustainable, and delicious ingredients that are also very versatile. This pasta dish highlights their subtle earthy flavors and takes that to the next level with a creamy, tomato-y twist. This meal comes together easily, it's affordable, and it'll satisfy just about anyone. At first, my mushroom pastas were done with a completely white sauce, but once I added tomato paste to this dish, I unlocked a completely new world of mushroom pasta. This is currently my favorite way to make it.

INSTRUCTIONS

Slice the mushrooms. Don't worry about getting them too thin because they will shrink in the pan. Leave some smaller mushrooms whole. This is really a matter of preference—you are the master of your mushroom sizes.

Pour a few generous swirls of olive oil into a large stainless-steel skillet, place it over medium-high heat, and heat the oil until it shimmers. If you don't have a stainless-steel skillet, use whatever you have, but add a little less oil. Add the mushrooms and a generous pinch of salt. Cook for 6 to 8 minutes, moving the mushrooms only occasionally. Toward the end of the cook time, they should start releasing some of their water. This is when you can start moving them a bit more, making sure every piece is cooked evenly.

Add the garlic and cook with the mushrooms for 1 to 2 minutes until softened and fragrant. Pour in the wine and cook to reduce for about 1 minute until a thicker sauce forms in the pan.

Stir in the tomato paste. Cook for 2 to 3 minutes to enhance the taste and aroma of the tomato paste. This is also when you can start cooking the pasta.

Cook the pasta in a large pot of salted water according to the package directions until al dente.

When the pasta starts cooking, stir the cream into the sauce, mixing thoroughly. Taste and add a small amount of salt; we can add more later. Simmer the sauce over medium heat until the pasta is cooked.

Using tongs, transfer the pasta to the sauce without shaking off any excess liquid. Keep the pasta water nearby in case you need more. Top the pasta with the parmesan and toss everything until a thick sauce forms and the pasta is thoroughly coated. Add small amounts of pasta water, if needed to loosen the sauce. Turn off the heat and finish with the chopped parsley. Season to taste with pepper, and more salt, if needed.

INGREDIENTS

8 ounces (225 g) mixed fresh mushrooms (anything you like, even just one affordable variety if on a budget)

Olive oil for coating the pan

Kosher salt

3 garlic cloves, minced

½ cup (120 ml) white wine, chicken broth, or water

2 tablespoons (32 g) tomato paste

4 ounces (115 g) dried pasta (I recommend tagliatelle)

1 cup (120 ml) heavy cream or low-fat cream (if you want fewer calories)

¼ cup (25 g) grated parmesan cheese

Big handful of chopped fresh parsley

Freshly cracked black pepper

ONE-POT CHICKEN AND BROCCOLI PASTA

YIELD: SERVES 2

A fun way to get some protein and eat your vegetables is with this unique risotto-style one-pot pasta. If you've made other pasta recipes from this chapter, you'll notice this technique is different, being more similar to a risotto: You'll cook the dried pasta directly in the pot with less liquid, eventually reducing that liquid to become the pasta sauce. This works because, as the pasta cooks, starch releases and is mixed into the liquid, resulting in a thick sauce that coats the pasta. This is by no means a high-effort recipe, but you'll have to put some attention into stirring the pasta and aiding this magical process (because science is magic).

INSTRUCTIONS

In a small saucepan over low heat, warm the chicken broth and keep it warm. You probably will not need the full amount, so you may have leftovers to sip.

While the broth heats, chop the broccoli florets into bite-size pieces.

Pro tip: *Save the broccoli stalk for Veggie Stock from Scraps (page 23), or thinly chop it for stir-fries.*

This is all going to happen in one pot. I use a Dutch oven, but you can use any deeper pot or pan, like a wok. Place the pot over medium-high heat and add 1 tablespoon (15 ml) of olive oil to thinly coat the bottom. Add the ground chicken and season it with salt and pepper. Cook the chicken for 3 to 4 minutes, breaking it up using a potato masher, wooden spoon, or spatula. Don't worry about size; we don't want this to be a fine mince. The goal is to get some browning and cook the chicken through until it is no longer pink. Transfer the cooked chicken to a bowl.

INGREDIENTS

3 to 4 cups (720 to 960 ml) chicken broth

1 medium-size head broccoli

2 tablespoons (30 ml) olive oil, divided

8 ounces (225 g) ground chicken

Kosher salt and ground black pepper

2 or 3 garlic cloves, sliced

1 fresh red chile, sliced, seeded for less heat

4 ounces (115 g) dried small pasta (I prefer orecchiette)

¼ cup (25 g) grated parmesan cheese

1 bunch fresh parsley, chopped

Grated zest of ½ lemon

Juice of ½ lemon

Return the pot to medium-high heat and add the remaining 1 tablespoon (15 ml) of olive oil, followed by the garlic and chile. Stir-fry for 1 minute.

Add the broccoli and cook for 3 to 4 minutes until it loses its raw edge; you don't want it to turn to mush. Bonus points if you get some browning on it. Transfer the veggies to the bowl with the chicken.

Turn the heat to medium and add the dried pasta to the pot, followed by enough hot chicken broth to just cover the pasta. Cook for 10 minutes, stirring every 30 seconds or so to help release and distribute that starch. The goal is to cook the pasta to al dente and reduce the liquid around it, forming a sauce. If things look dry, add more stock.

When the pasta is cooked, turn the heat to low and add the parmesan cheese, parsley, lemon zest, and lemon juice. Stir the pasta until a thick, homogenous sauce coats it. Turn off the heat and season with salt and pepper to taste.

CHEAP CHICKEN POKE BOWL

YIELD: SERVES 1

Poke bowls originated in Hawaii, but they have since gained a lot of global popularity as a healthy alternative to other take-out meals. I love them. I get them a lot, but every single time I think to myself, *This is ridiculously expensive.* I wanted to replicate the poke experience at home, for a small fraction of the cost, using fresh, inexpensive ingredients and applying some basic techniques. Keep in mind, this is by no means an authentic poke bowl—we're not even using fish—but we're building the dish with the poke format in mind.

INGREDIENTS FOR CHICKEN:

1 boneless, skinless chicken breast

2 tablespoons (30 ml) soy sauce

2 teaspoons rice vinegar

1 teaspoon toasted sesame oil

1 scallion, white and green parts, chopped

2 garlic cloves, minced

½ fresh red chile, finely chopped, seeded for less heat

INGREDIENTS FOR BOWL:

¾ cup (150 g) raw sushi rice

1 tablespoon (15 ml) vegetable oil, divided

1 cup (130 g) frozen peas

1 garlic clove, minced

1 teaspoon red pepper flakes

Handful of chopped fresh cilantro

Squeeze of fresh lemon juice

Handful of pickled carrots (see Pickled Red Onions and Other Things, page 24)

¼ English cucumber, diced and generously salted

Kosher salt

3 surimi (imitation crab) sticks, chopped into bite-size pieces

INGREDIENTS FOR DRESSING:

2 tablespoons (30 g) mayonnaise

1 teaspoon wasabi paste

Squeeze of fresh lemon juice

1 to 2 teaspoons water

INSTRUCTIONS

To make the chicken: Cut the chicken into bite-size cubes and place it in a small container. Add the soy sauce, rice vinegar, sesame oil, scallion, garlic, and chile. Thoroughly mix until the chicken is well coated with the marinade. Top with a tightly fitting lid and keep refrigerated until use, or for up to 1 day.

To start the bowl: In a fine-mesh sieve, wash the rice, then cook it according to the package directions. If you have a rice cooker, use that: In it, simply combine equal parts rice and water and turn on the cooker—that's it. In a few minutes you'll have perfectly cooked rice.

While the chicken marinates and the rice cooks, prep the remaining ingredients.

To make the dressing: In a small bowl, stir together the mayonnaise, wasabi, lemon juice, and a touch of water to thin the mixture to a dressing consistency.

To finish the bowl: In a large skillet over medium-high heat, heat 1½ teaspoons of vegetable oil until it shimmers. Add the frozen peas and cook for 1 to 2 minutes. Stir in the garlic, red pepper flakes, cilantro, and lemon juice until thoroughly distributed. Transfer to a bowl and return the skillet to medium-high heat.

Pour the remaining 1½ teaspoons of vegetable oil into the skillet and heat until it shimmers. Remove the chicken from the marinade, shaking off any excess, and add it to the hot oil. Cook the chicken for 4 to 5 minutes, flipping every piece occasionally to ensure even cooking on all sides.

To assemble the bowl: I start with a bed of rice, then add all my ingredients in their own little corner, but you can do it in any way you like. Add the chicken, peas, pickled carrots, cucumber, and surimi. Top with some wasabi mayo, and you've just made an affordable, nutritious, and delicious meal.

EPIC TOFU BURRITO BOWL

YIELD: SERVES 1

As a European who has never been to the United States, I've always been very curious about restaurants like Chipotle. I see their burritos and their bowls everywhere on the internet, and it occupies this weird place in my brain of food that I would, hypothetically, like but will not taste in the near future. One day, however, I realized I can just do it myself, and it's probably going to be better and healthier. My protein of choice for this is usually tofu, but feel free to sub chicken breast.

INGREDIENTS FOR RICE:

½ cup (100 g) raw rice

1 tablespoon (15 ml) olive oil

1 small bunch fresh cilantro, chopped

Kosher salt

Grated zest of ½ lime

Juice of ½ lime

INGREDIENTS FOR TOFU:

1½ tablespoons (23 ml) olive oil

4 to 6 ounces (115 to 170 g) firm tofu

1 teaspoon smoked paprika

1 teaspoon ground cumin

1 teaspoon garlic powder

1 teaspoon onion powder

½ teaspoon cayenne pepper

Kosher salt

INGREDIENTS FOR BLACK BEANS:

1 tablespoon (15 ml) olive oil

½ cup (115 g) canned black beans, drained, not rinsed

2 garlic cloves, minced

1 teaspoon ground cumin

1 teaspoon smoked paprika

Kosher salt

INGREDIENTS FOR CORN SALSA:

½ cup (78 g) fresh or canned corn

1 Roma tomato, diced

½ yellow onion, finely diced

Kosher salt

INGREDIENTS FOR SERVING (OPTIONAL):

Guacamole (see Easier Than Taco Bell Tacos, page 96)

1 tablespoon (15 g) sour cream or full-fat plain Greek yogurt or vegan alternative

Hot sauce

INSTRUCTIONS

Phew, I know you're probably overwhelmed by all the ingredients, but trust me, it's not as difficult as it looks. There's a lot of assembling, but not a lot of cooking.

First, the rice: In a fine-mesh sieve, wash the rice, then cook it according to the package directions. If you have a rice cooker, use that: In it, simply combine equal parts rice and water and turn on the cooker—that's it. In a few minutes you'll have perfectly cooked rice. Transfer the rice to a bowl, then add the olive oil, cilantro, salt to taste, and the lime zest and juice. Mix thoroughly and you have a simple, flavorful cilantro-lime rice.

To make the tofu: In a medium-size skillet over medium heat, heat 1 tablespoon (15 ml) of olive oil until it shimmers. Using your clean hands, crumble the tofu into the skillet into differently sized chunks—don't worry about being precise.

Toss the tofu in the oil and cook for 6 to 8 minutes, stirring occasionally, until some pieces start to crisp up. Pour in the remaining ½ tablespoon (8 ml) of olive oil and toss the tofu to coat.

Add the smoked paprika, cumin, garlic powder, onion powder, cayenne, and salt to taste. Toss to coat the tofu pieces with the spices and cook for 3 to 4 minutes until slightly browned and crispy.

To make the black beans: In a small saucepan or skillet over medium, heat the olive oil until it shimmers. Add the black beans and cook for 3 to 4 minutes,

stirring constantly, until most of the liquid is gone and some of the beans have split. Stir in the garlic, cumin, paprika, and salt to taste.

To make the corn salsa: In a medium-size bowl, combine all the corn salsa ingredients and thoroughly mix with a spoon. Sometimes, simpler is better.

To assemble your bowl: Place the cilantro rice in the center of the bowl and layer the other elements around it: tofu, black beans, and corn salsa. I also like to serve it with guacamole and sour cream and cover it in hot sauce.

LOADED VEGGIE QUINOA BOWL

YIELD: SERVES 2

This might be the freshest, most veggie-packed recipe in this book. It combines healthy grains, cooked and raw veggies, and lots of layers of flavor, texture, and nutrients. This is a dish you can make in bulk and store in the fridge for 3 to 4 days, and have a nutritious and delicious side (or main) dish for pretty much the whole work week. It's the kind of food that makes me feel happy throughout the day when I eat it.

INSTRUCTIONS

Preheat the oven to 400°F (200°C, or gas mark 6). Line a baking sheet with parchment paper.

Chop the broccoli florets into bite-size pieces and place them in a large bowl.

Pro tip: *Save the broccoli stalk for Veggie Stock from Scraps (page 23), or thinly chop it for stir-fries.*

To that same bowl add the chopped sweet potato and yellow onion slices. Hit these veggies with 2 tablespoons (30 ml) of olive oil and a generous pinch of salt. Toss to coat and arrange them on the prepared baking sheet, spreading them out as evenly as possible. Reserve the bowl. Bake for 20 to 25 minutes until the veggies have slightly browned and softened (it's okay to get a little char).

In the reserved bowl, combine the cooked quinoa, roasted veggies, cherry tomatoes, chopped parsley, walnuts, lemon juice, and the remaining 1 tablespoon (15 ml) of olive oil. Thoroughly toss together until all the veggies are evenly distributed. Taste and season with salt and pepper, as needed. Add more lemon juice if you feel the dish lacks a kick.

INGREDIENTS

1 medium-size head broccoli

1 large sweet potato, unpeeled, cut into bite-size pieces

1 yellow onion, sliced

3 tablespoons (45 ml) olive oil, divided

2 cups (370 g) cooked quinoa

Kosher salt and ground black pepper

1 cup (150 g) quartered cherry tomatoes

1 large bunch fresh parsley, chopped

½ cup (60 g) chopped walnuts

Juice of ½ lemon, plus more as needed

CREAMY CHICKPEA CURRY

YIELD: SERVES 2

Sometimes, I get home after a busy day and realize I don't really have a lot to work with in my fridge. That's usually when I turn to this chickpea curry because I pretty much always have a can of chickpeas in my pantry, as well as all the other ingredients. This comes together easily, it's super satisfying, and it's vegan. I use some shortcuts in this recipe because I want this to be a low-effort dish, but you can certainly improve it by using your own blend of spices or cooking the chickpeas from scratch, but let's be honest, you bought this book for a reason—you're not gonna do that (but I'll cheer you on if you do!).

INGREDIENTS

2 tablespoons (30 ml) neutral oil

1 yellow onion, finely diced

2 garlic cloves, minced

1 fresh red chile, finely sliced, seeded for less heat

Kosher salt

1 tablespoon (6 g) curry powder

1 (15-ounce, or 425 g) can chickpeas, drained and rinsed

2 tablespoons (32 g) tomato paste

1 cup (240 ml) full-fat coconut milk

Cooked rice for serving (optional)

Fresh cilantro for topping

Lime wedges for garnish

INSTRUCTIONS

In a heavy-bottomed pot, such as a Dutch oven, over medium heat, heat the neutral oil until it shimmers. Add the onion, garlic, sliced chile, and a generous pinch of salt to the hot oil. This is an important step in this curry: We cook the onion a bit longer until it turns soft and slightly caramelized. So, cook for 8 to 10 minutes until that happens, stirring every 30 seconds or so.

Stir in the curry powder until well combined. Cook for 1 to 2 minutes, stirring constantly, to bring out the flavors of the spice blend.

Add the chickpeas and tomato paste and stir them into the mixture, cooking for 1 minute, just until the chickpeas are well coated with the spices and the paste is distributed well.

Pour in the coconut milk and mix thoroughly. Simmer over medium heat for 5 to 6 minutes, stirring constantly, until the curry is thick. Taste and season with salt. Turn off the heat.

I serve this curry with rice, top it with fresh cilantro, and squeeze lime wedges over the top to finish with some brightness.

CHAPTER 7:

PARTY ESSENTIALS

A house party with no food is like my pantry without seven cans of bean varieties: incomplete. These recipes are guaranteed to make all your guests like you a little bit more.

CROWD PLEASERS

Perfect Smash Burgers   140

Straightforward Black Bean Tacos   143

Spicy Cheesy Quesadillas   146

FINGER FOODS

Buffalo Cauliflower Bites   148

Oven-Baked Chicken Tenders   151

Parm-Crusted Potato Wedges   152

My Favorite Veggie Fritters   155

PERFECT SMASH BURGERS

YIELD: SERVES 4

This is probably what I make most often when I have guests over and I don't want to put that much effort into cooking. The process is free, imprecise, and fun. As long as you follow some basic techniques and principles, the results will be mouthwatering. The patties are smashed over high heat to maximize the cooking surface and develop a flavorful crust, because the crispy crust is the best part. Double or triple this recipe according to the number of guests and how hungry they are. Have fun!

INSTRUCTIONS

Smash burgers are best when they're fresh and piping hot, so before we cook them, it's best to have everything prepped.

To make the sauce: In a small bowl, stir together all the sauce ingredients thoroughly until everything is combined.

To make the burgers: Use a cast-iron or stainless-steel skillet or griddle for frying. If you only have a nonstick pan, just use less oil.

In a skillet over medium-high heat, melt the butter. Add the diced onions and a sprinkle of salt and cook for about 4 minutes, stirring occasionally, until well browned. Transfer the onions to a plate.

Return the skillet to the heat and place the buns halves, cut-side down, in it. Toast them thoroughly for 1 to 2 minutes. Remove from the skillet and turn the heat to high.

Divide the ground beef into 4 (4-ounce, or 115 g) portions and roll each into a ball (there are a lot of ball references, so stay with me). Generously season the tops of the beef balls with salt. Pour a few generous swirls of olive oil into the skillet and heat it until it smokes. Add the beef balls, salted-side down. Using a wide

INGREDIENTS FOR SAUCE:

½ cup (120 g) mayonnaise

1 tablespoon (15 g) mustard

1 tablespoon (15 g) ketchup

1 tablespoon (15 g) finely minced pickle

½ yellow onion, finely minced

1 teaspoon lime salt

1 teaspoon ground black pepper

½ teaspoon kosher salt

INGREDIENTS FOR BURGER:

1 tablespoon (14 g) butter

2 yellow onions, diced

Kosher salt

4 brioche or potato burger buns, split

1 pound (454 g) 80/20 ground beef

Olive oil for frying

4 slices cheddar cheese, or other melty cheese

1 large tomato, sliced and salted

Shredded lettuce for topping

Sliced pickles for topping

spatula, press down on the balls to flatten them into thin patties. You should hear an aggressive sizzle—that's a good sign!

Pro tip: *If your spatula needs more pressure, use the back of a wooden spoon to apply targeted pressure.*

Generously season the top of the patties with salt. Cook for 90 seconds to 2 minutes without disturbing. Flip the patties using a spatula, scraping up as much of the crust from the bottom as you can, because that's where the flavor is. After flipping, immediately hit each patty with a slice of cheddar and cook until the cheese melts. If you're looking for the best melt and don't mind processed cheese, use American cheese.

To assemble the burgers: Spread some sauce on the bottom bun, top with shredded lettuce, the hot, cheesy patty, more sauce on top of it, tomato, browned onions, pickles, and finally, crown it with the top bun.

STRAIGHTFORWARD BLACK BEAN TACOS

YIELD: SERVES 4

From my experience, just hearing the word "taco" can make anyone happy, so I can't think of anything better to serve to a large group of friends than this meal. I put together a very straightforward one-pan taco filling that's richly packed with nutrients and flavor that anyone can make. I pair the tacos with yogurt avocado crema to add a little freshness and tang, and the result is as easy as putting those two things together inside a tortilla.

INGREDIENTS FOR TACOS:

2 tablespoons (30 ml) olive oil

1 yellow onion, diced

3 garlic cloves, minced

1 green bell pepper, diced

1 (16-ounce, or 454 g) can black beans, drained and rinsed

1 (1-ounce, or 28 g) packet taco seasoning

1 ear fresh corn, husked, kernels cut from the cob

Kosher salt

8 to 10 (6-inch, or 15 cm) flour tortillas, warmed

Crumbled feta cheese for topping

Pickled red onions (see Pickled Red Onions and Other Things, page 24) for topping

INGREDIENTS FOR AVOCADO CREMA:

2 avocados, halved and pitted

1 garlic clove, sliced

Grated zest of 1 lime

Juice of 1 lime

1 bunch fresh cilantro

1 jalapeño pepper, sliced, seeded for less heat

2 tablespoons (30 g) full-fat plain Greek yogurt

1 tablespoon (15 ml) olive oil

Kosher salt

INSTRUCTIONS

To make the filling: In a large skillet over medium heat, heat the olive oil until it shimmers. Add the diced onion and minced garlic and stir-fry for 2 to 3 minutes until slightly softened and browned. Add the diced green bell pepper. Continue stir-frying for 3 to 4 minutes until the bell pepper loses its raw edge.

Stir in the black beans and taco seasoning. Cook for 5 minutes, stirring occasionally. You want to get rid of some of the moisture in the beans and have all the ingredients get to know each other and stick together a bit better. Feel free to smash some of the beans using the back of your spatula or wooden spoon.

Fold the corn into the filling. Taste the filling and season with salt, as needed. Turn the heat to the lowest setting to keep warm until serving.

To make the avocado crema: Scoop the avocado flesh into a blender and add the remaining crema ingredients, including salt to taste. Blend until a smooth, thick sauce forms. If the crema looks too stiff, loosen it with a splash of water.

Assemble the tacos according to your preference, but I use avocado crema as the base of the taco, add the black bean filling on top of that, and finish with some feta crumbles and pickled onion.

SPICY CHEESY QUESADILLAS

YIELD: SERVES 4

Crispy quesadillas deliver satisfying cheesiness for feeding a hungry crowd, and they're easy and quick to make. I pair the cheesiness with a roasted jalapeño and garlic salsa for a deep sweet and savory flavor with a kick of heat. You can make the salsa ahead and refrigerate it for up to 5 days, but I promise it won't last that long.

INGREDIENTS FOR SALSA:

8 to 10 jalapeño peppers (depending on size), halved, seeded for less heat

1 yellow onion, quartered

4 or 5 garlic cloves, unpeeled

Olive oil for coating and blending

Kosher salt

Juice of 1 lime

INGREDIENTS FOR QUESADILLAS:

1 cup (115 g) shredded cheddar cheese

½ cup (60 g) shredded Gruyère cheese

½ cup (58 g) shredded Monterey Jack or Gouda cheese

4 large (10-inch, or 25 cm) flour tortillas

Olive oil for brushing

INSTRUCTIONS

Preheat the oven to 400°F (200°C, or gas mark 6). Line a sheet pan with parchment paper.

To make the salsa: On the prepared pan, combine the jalapeño halves, onion, and garlic cloves. Drizzle with olive oil and sprinkle with salt. Bake for 15 to 20 minutes, or until the jalapeño skins are slightly charred and separate from the peppers.

Carefully pop the garlic cloves from their skins into a blender and add the remaining roasted veggies and lime juice. Season with salt. Blend until relatively smooth. With the blender running, drizzle in 2 to 3 tablespoons (30 to 45 ml) of olive oil until the sauce is fully emulsified (with a creamy, thick consistency). If it's too thick, blend in a splash of water.

To make the quesadillas: In a large bowl, toss together the cheeses using your clean hands until evenly distributed.

Place the tortillas on a work surface. Spread a generous handful of cheese on half of a tortilla, covering the entire half. Spread a generous layer of jalapeño salsa on the other half. Fold one side over the other and brush the top lightly with olive oil.

Place the quesadilla in a cold 12-inch (30 cm) skillet, oiled-side down (you should be able to fit two). Turn the heat under the skillet to medium and cook the tortillas for about 2½ minutes until golden brown. Carefully flip the tortillas and cook the other side for 1 to 2 minutes, making sure not to burn them. Cut the quesadillas into triangles and serve.

Repeat with the remaining tortillas, cheese, and salsa.

BUFFALO CAULIFLOWER BITES

YIELD: SERVES 4 TO 6

Meat eater or no, these buffalo cauliflower bites will impress. You wouldn't think this much satisfying flavor and texture could come from cauliflower, but these bites are borderline addictive and will convince even your most carnivorous friends to appreciate a meatless bite. They're baked instead of fried to reduce calories, especially since they're coated in a butter-heavy sauce.

INSTRUCTIONS

Preheat the oven to 400°F (200°C, or gas mark 6). Line a sheet pan with parchment paper.

To make the bites: Remove the stem by cutting around it with a paring knife. Using your hands or a knife, separate the cauliflower into florets. I like a combination of big chunks cut with my knife and individual florets torn with my hands. Place the cauliflower in a large bowl, leaving the crumbles behind.

In another large bowl, whisk the flour, cornstarch, garlic powder, and remaining seasonings to blend, then gradually whisk in the water until the batter is loose, about the consistency of pancake batter. You may not need all the water.

Place the cauliflower pieces in the batter and use your clean hands to toss until every piece is well coated. Transfer the coated bites to the prepared pan. Bake for 20 minutes until pale golden in color; they will not be fully cooked.

To make the sauce: While the cauliflower bakes, in a saucepan over medium heat, bring the hot sauce to a simmer and cook for 5 minutes, stirring constantly. Add the

INGREDIENTS FOR BITES:

1 head cauliflower

1 cup (120 g) all-purpose flour

½ cup (64 g) cornstarch

2 teaspoons garlic powder

1 teaspoon kosher salt

1 teaspoon baking powder

1 teaspoon smoked paprika

1 teaspoon cayenne pepper

1 teaspoon dried thyme

1 to 1½ cups (240 to 360 ml) water

INGREDIENTS FOR SAUCE:

¾ cup (180 ml) hot sauce
(I use Frank's)

2 tablespoons (28 g) butter

3 tablespoons (45 ml) distilled white vinegar

Herby Yogurt Dip (page 26) for serving

butter and let it melt into the sauce while stirring until the sauce thickens. Stir in the vinegar and remove the pan from the heat.

Immediately transfer the cauliflower bites to a large bowl (keep the oven on and reserve the sheet pan). Pour on a generous amount of sauce (don't add it all at once, to avoid oversaucing) and toss until the bites are coated thoroughly.

Transfer the sauced-up cauliflower back to the sheet pan and bake for 20 minutes until the bites have a gentle crispiness and a red-brownish color. Serve with the dip and watch them disappear.

OVEN-BAKED CHICKEN TENDERS

YIELD: SERVES 4

A good chicken tender is hard to beat, so forget about those frozen chicken fingers that turn dry 1.7 seconds after you take them out of the oven. This recipe gives you easy-to-make, crispy but still juicy chicken tenders. Not only is baking these a healthier option, but the hands-off approach is better and more convenient than dealing with a pot of hot oil. I serve them with barbecue sauce and a simple side salad.

INGREDIENTS

1½ pounds (681 g) chicken tenders

Kosher salt and ground black pepper

1 large egg

2 large egg whites

1 cup (120 g) all-purpose flour

¼ cup (32 g) cornstarch

2 teaspoons smoked paprika

2 teaspoons garlic powder

1 teaspoon salt

1 teaspoon dried thyme

2 cups (56 g) crushed cornflakes

½ cup (50 g) grated parmesan cheese

INSTRUCTIONS

Preheat the oven to 425°F (220°C or gas mark 7). Place a wire rack over a baking sheet.

I season the chicken tenders. I find this provides an extra layer of flavor that can be lacking under the crust. Simply sprinkle some salt and pepper on all the tenders and press the seasonings down using clean hands.

In a shallow bowl or dish, whisk the egg and egg whites to blend. The egg whites are high in protein and will produce a crispier coating.

In another shallow bowl or dish, stir together the flour, cornstarch, paprika, garlic powder, 1 teaspoon of salt, and the thyme until well distributed. This is the flour dredge. In a third bowl, mix the crushed cornflakes and grated parmesan cheese. This provides a final layer or crunchiness with a savory punch.

Coat a batch of seasoned tenders in the flour dredge. Shake off any excess flour and immediately transfer the tenders to the egg wash. Using your hands, make sure the tenders are thoroughly coated and transfer them to the cornflake mixture, not shaking off any excess egg. Press the cornflake parmesan mixture into the tenders to ensure they're thoroughly coated, then transfer them to the wire rack. Repeat with the remaining tenders.

Bake the tenders on the rack for 16 to 20 minutes, flipping halfway through the baking time, until they develop a golden-brown crust.

PARM-CRUSTED POTATO WEDGES

YIELD: SERVES 4

Potatoes are normally served as a side dish, but this recipe makes them the star of the show. These wedges are coated in a crispy, spiced-up crust, and they're wonderfully soft on the inside. The parmesan provides an extra kick of earthy, savory flavor that works so well with the potatoes. I promise you a batch of these will be gone in minutes, especially if you serve them with a sour cream and scallion dip (see Pro tip).

INGREDIENTS

1 large egg

3 large egg whites

3 garlic cloves, minced

1½ cups (150 g) freshly grated parmesan cheese

½ cup (58 g) bread crumbs

1 teaspoon kosher salt

1 teaspoon ground black pepper

1 teaspoon dried thyme

1 teaspoon dried oregano

1 teaspoon smoked paprika

1 teaspoon garlic powder

6 to 8 large potatoes, unpeeled, cut into wedges

INSTRUCTIONS

Preheat the oven to 350°F (180°C, or gas mark 4). Line a baking sheet with parchment paper.

In a shallow bowl or dish, whisk the egg, egg whites, and garlic until thoroughly combined to create the egg wash. In another shallow bowl or dish, stir together the parmesan, bread crumbs, and all the seasonings until mixed.

One at a time, coat each potato wedge in the egg wash and then in the parmesan mixture until well coated on all sides and place on the prepared baking sheet, skin-side down. Bake for 40 minutes until crisp and golden brown outside and tender inside.

Pro tip: *To make the sour cream and scallion dip, in a small bowl, stir together ¼ cup (60 g) of sour cream, 1 scallion (white and green parts, finely sliced), and a handful of chopped fresh dill until thoroughly combined. Taste and season with salt.*

MY FAVORITE VEGGIE FRITTERS

YIELD: SERVES 4

Making veggie fritters is one of my favorite ways to use leftover vegetables. I never really measure the quantities in this recipe because it's forgiving and adjustable. I like that because I don't have to think about it too much to make a delicious party snack packed with vegetable goodness. When you bite into one of these fritters, you'll break through a crispy, salty exterior to reach a satisfying bite of flavorful vegetables. These are my favorite vegetables to use, but feel free to use others, like broccoli, corn, or potatoes. Serve with a dip of yogurt, a squeeze of lime juice, and a sprinkle of fresh chives.

INSTRUCTIONS

In a large bowl, combine the carrots, zucchini, sweet potato, and a generous sprinkle of salt. Mix the vegetables thoroughly. Let sit for 10 minutes. During this time, a lot of the moisture will leave the vegetables, which is important, because the drier the veggies, the crispier the fritter. Squeeze out the excess moisture over a sink and transfer the vegetables back to a dry bowl.

Add the remaining ingredients to the bowl, except the oil, and thoroughly mix until a cohesive batter forms. You want a mixture that sticks together and is thick enough to be scooped. If things look too thick, add a splash of water until you reach the desired consistency.

Place a large skillet over medium heat and pour in enough vegetable oil to coat the bottom of the pan. Heat the oil until it shimmers. Using a ¼-cup measure, scoop dollops of batter into the hot oil. Gently flatten them. Cook for 3 to 4 minutes per side until golden brown. Transfer the fritters to a wire rack and season immediately with a sprinkle of salt on both sides. Repeat with the remaining batter.

INGREDIENTS

2 medium-size carrots, grated

1 medium-size zucchini, grated

1 medium-size sweet potato, peeled and grated

Kosher salt

2 scallions, white and green parts, thinly sliced

2 garlic cloves, minced

1 bunch fresh cilantro, chopped

1 large egg

½ cup (60 g) all-purpose flour

¼ cup (32 g) cornstarch

1 teaspoon baking powder

Vegetable oil for frying

CHAPTER 8:

SWEETS AND TREATS

Let me remind you of something: You deserve a treat! Honestly, what's life without dessert? In this chapter, you'll find satisfying sweet treats with a nutritious twist so you can ditch the guilt (mainly).

DESSERTS

Healthier Chocolate
Lava Cake   158

Two-Ingredient Banana
Soft-Serve   161

Cinnamon Apple Crumble 162

My Mom's Walnut Dessert
Pasta   165

Avocado Chocolate
Mousse   166

SWEET TOOTH SNACKS

Yogurt Parfait   167

PB&J Frozen Yogurt Bark 168

My Favorite Cookie:
Banana Oatmeal   171

HEALTHIER CHOCOLATE LAVA CAKE

YIELD: SERVES 2

There aren't many better feelings than cutting into a molten lava cake, revealing the hot, decadent, chocolatey inside slowly oozing onto your spoon. I tried re-creating this experience with slightly more nutritionally balanced ingredients many times, and I think this recipe is the ideal version. It has a deep, dark chocolate undertone that compensates for the lack of sugar, creating a satisfying dessert experience. Orange zest and sea salt enhance the cocoa flavors, but you can leave those out if you're not a fan. Serve with yogurt, berries, fruit jam, nuts, or all.

INGREDIENTS FOR FILLING:

2 tablespoons (33 g) grated dark chocolate (70 percent cacao or more)

1 tablespoon (14 g) coconut oil

INGREDIENTS FOR CAKE:

Coconut oil for preparing the ramekins

1 large egg

1 tablespoon (14 g) brown sugar or (12.5 g) granulated sugar

1 tablespoon (15 g) applesauce

Splash of milk or plant-based milk, plus more as needed

¼ cup (30 g) oat flour (ground oats)

2 tablespoons (10 g) high-quality cocoa powder

½ teaspoon baking powder

Pinch of sea salt

1 teaspoon grated orange zest

INSTRUCTIONS

To make the filling: In a small microwave-safe bowl, combine the dark chocolate and coconut oil. Microwave on high power in 30-second increments, stirring after each, until a glossy chocolate mixture forms. Transfer to the freezer for at least 10 minutes.

Preheat the oven to 400°F (200°C, or gas mark 6). Brush two 4-ounce (120 ml) ramekins with a layer of coconut oil. This will ensure the cakes do not stick to the ramekins.

To make the cake: In a medium-size bowl, combine the egg and brown sugar. With a whisk, whip the mixture until slightly foamy and the sugar is fully incorporated. Whisk in the applesauce and milk until incorporated. These are your wet ingredients.

Sift the oat flour, cocoa powder, baking powder, and salt into the wet ingredients. Add the orange zest and whisk until a thick batter forms. If the batter is too thick, add another splash of milk to loosen it up.

Evenly divide half of the batter between the prepared ramekins. Place half of the now-solidified chocolate filling in the center of each ramekin. Top the filling with the remaining batter, dividing it evenly. Bake for 10 to 12 minutes until the cakes are set and slightly puffed.

Let the cakes cool in the ramekins for 2 to 3 minutes until you can handle them with a kitchen towel. Use a knife to carefully separate the cake from the walls of the ramekins and invert the ramekins onto plates. Tap the bottom a few times with the back of a spoon and gently lift the ramekin to reveal the lava cake.

TWO-INGREDIENT BANANA SOFT-SERVE

YIELD: SERVES 2

This might sound crazy, but I actually like this banana soft-serve more than most regular ice creams. The banana has such an intense natural creaminess that you can create the most delightful soft-serve by just blending it up when it's frozen. It also has an amazing natural sweetness that pairs so well with the deep cocoa flavor, especially if you use overripe bananas (spot-on use for leftovers by the way). And, by the way, that's literally all you need: bananas and cocoa powder.

INSTRUCTIONS

Slice the bananas and place them in a zip-top plastic bag. Seal the bag and freeze for at least 6 hours.

Place the frozen bananas in a blender, breaking off the pieces as best you can. Blend on high speed, using the blender tamper to occasionally scrape the sides and help the mixture blend better. At first, the blending process will be a bit difficult but eventually everything will come together in a firm, creamy mixture.

Add the cocoa powder and salt (if using). Blend on high speed until the cocoa is incorporated.

I top this with some chopped nuts and a drizzle of honey.

INGREDIENTS

3 or 4 large overripe bananas

2 tablespoons (10 g) high-quality cocoa powder

Pinch of flaky sea salt (optional)

Chopped nuts for topping

Drizzle of honey for topping

CINNAMON APPLE CRUMBLE

YIELD: SERVES 4

My favorite dessert is that hot slice of apple pie topped with a cold, melty scoop of vanilla ice cream. I figured out a way to enjoy these same flavors in a much more nutritious way in this apple crumble that comes together quickly. And I'm not gonna lie—I top this with a scoop of ice cream because I DESERVE A LITTLE FUN, OKAY? Also, this is wonderful the next day— just pop it in the fridge and treat yourself to a cold snack.

INSTRUCTIONS

Preheat the oven to 350°F (180°C, or gas mark 4).

To make the filling: In a large bowl, combine the apples and remaining filling ingredients. Use your clean hands to mix everything thoroughly until the apples are well coated. Transfer the apple mixture and the juices to a 9 × 13-inch (23 × 33 cm) glass baking dish. Reserve the bowl. Bake for 10 minutes until the apples soften slightly.

To make the oat topping: In the reserved bowl, combine all the topping ingredients and mix them using your hands to thoroughly distribute the coconut oil across the dry ingredients. You should get some texture variation, like bigger chunks of crumbled-up oats and biscuits. Sprinkle the topping over the baked apples, getting some between the apple slices and down to the bottom of the baking dish. Lightly press down on the topping to even out the layer. This will allow the top to crisp up nicely.

Return to the oven for up to 15 minutes, or until the top is slightly browned and the apples have fully softened.

Serve hot topped with the vanilla ice cream, or let cool for 10 minutes before digging in.

INGREDIENTS FOR APPLE FILLING:

4 red apples, thinly sliced

2 tablespoons (40 g) maple syrup or honey

Juice of ½ lemon

1 teaspoon rum extract or rum flavoring

1 tablespoon (8 g) cornstarch

1 teaspoon ground cinnamon

½ teaspoon ground nutmeg

INGREDIENTS FOR OAT TOPPING:

1¼ cups (100 g) old-fashioned rolled oats

½ cup (50 g) crushed digestive biscuits (about 4 biscuits) or (60 g) graham cracker crumbs

¼ cup (30 g) chopped walnuts

2 tablespoons (28 g) coconut oil

2 tablespoons (40 g) maple syrup or honey

1 teaspoon ground cinnamon

1 teaspoon kosher salt

Vanilla ice cream or full-fat plain Greek yogurt for serving

INGREDIENTS

Kosher salt

4 to 6 ounces (115 to 170 g) dried tagliatelle pasta

1 cup (80 g) ground walnuts

½ cup (100 g) granulated sugar

½ cup (115 g) packed dark brown sugar

1 tablespoon (14 g) butter

MY MOM'S WALNUT DESSERT PASTA

YIELD: SERVES 2

Okay, not gonna lie. Ain't nothing nutritious about this. But, to me, healthy also means treating yourself occasionally, and this is a very special recipe to me. My mom used to make this for me as a kid, and she learned it from her mom, and it's been passed through generations. And here's the thing: I haven't really seen this anywhere else except when I talk to people from my home country of Romania.

So, it's time for me to put this recipe out into the world, so other people can experience it. It might sound weird at first, but I need you to be open, okay? Also, my mom made it clear that she never ever measures the ingredients, so adjust the amounts according to how you're feeling. Shout-out to my mom for being amazing, and for that matter, shout-out to my dad as well. Love you!

INSTRUCTIONS

Cook the pasta in a large pot of salted water according to the package directions until al dente.

While the pasta cooks, in a medium-size bowl, stir together the walnuts, granulated sugar, and brown sugar until well mixed.

In a skillet over medium-low heat, melt the butter until it bubbles.

As soon as the pasta reaches al dente, use tongs to pull it from the cooking water and add it to the skillet. Toss the pasta with the butter until well coated.

Add some walnut sugar to the pasta. I can't really tell you how much—just go with what you're feeling. Think about it as parmesan cheese on naked pasta. I add a liberal dash across the whole pan to make sure all the noodles are covered thoroughly. Toss and stir the pasta until

the sugar melts slightly and combines with the butter, forming a glossy, sugary "sauce."

Transfer the pasta into a serving dish and sprinkle it with more walnut sugar for some crunch. Serve hot.

You will probably have some leftover magic walnut sugar. Sprinkle it on oatmeal or buttered toast.

AVOCADO CHOCOLATE MOUSSE

YIELD: SERVES 2

I got this idea when I was browsing TikTok one day and saw a recipe that used avocado as a base for chocolate cake icing, and it blew my mind. Apparently using avocado in desserts is a thing, and after testing it, I can safely say the results do not taste like avocado but, instead, are naturally rich, creamy, and glossy. And those three words remind me of one thing: chocolate mousse. I also use a banana for added sweetness and creaminess, and top everything with chopped pistachios because, well, I want to maintain the green theme.

INGREDIENTS

3 ounces (85 g) dark chocolate

1 large ripe avocado, halved and pitted

1 banana

1 tablespoon (5 g) cocoa powder

2 tablespoons (40 g) honey

Chopped pistachios for topping

Shaved dark chocolate for topping

INSTRUCTIONS

In a small microwave-safe bowl, microwave the dark chocolate on high power in 30-second increments, stirring between each until the chocolate is fully melted. Transfer to a blender.

Scoop the avocado flesh into the blender with the chocolate and add the banana, cocoa powder, and honey. Blend until smooth, thick, rich, and velvety. Transfer to a small glass or ramekin and refrigerate for at least 2 hours, but ideally overnight.

Top with chopped pistachios and chocolate shavings to serve.

YOGURT PARFAIT

YIELD: SERVES 1

This is my go-to weeknight dessert. It's super nutritious and super satisfying. I was hesitant to even call this a parfait because it's really just a yogurt and fruit concoction I created. I pair the tangy, sweet yogurt base with creamy banana and a sweet-and-sour berry mixture, then top it with a crunchy layer of fruit and nuts for the finish.

INGREDIENTS

1 ripe banana

¼ cup (60 g) full-fat plain Greek yogurt

1 tablespoon (20 g) maple syrup or honey

1 teaspoon vanilla extract

Handful of fresh blueberries

Handful of fresh raspberries

Grated zest of ½ lemon

Juice of ½ lemon

1 teaspoon sugar

Dried cranberries for topping

Almond flakes or chopped walnuts for topping

INSTRUCTIONS

In a medium-size bowl, mash the banana with a fork. Don't worry about being too thorough; you want some chunks.

Add the yogurt, maple syrup, and vanilla and whisk vigorously for 1 to 2 minutes to incorporate some air and distribute the ingredients.

In a small bowl, gently stir together the blueberries, raspberries, lemon zest, lemon juice, and sugar. Let sit for 5 minutes.

In a small jar or glass, layer one-third of the yogurt mixture at the bottom, followed by half of the berries. Repeat this process for the next layer and finish with the last layer of yogurt. Top with dried fruit and nuts. Refrigerate for at least 30 minutes, but ideally overnight, before serving.

PB&J FROZEN YOGURT BARK

YIELD: SERVES 4

This frozen treat is a bonus on a hot summer day when you're looking for something refreshing, nutritious, and satisfying. It's also a terrific make-ahead snack, as you can make it, freeze it, and keep it for a looong time, although mine never lasts longer than one week because I eat it all.

INSTRUCTIONS

Line a baking sheet with parchment paper. In a large bowl, stir together the yogurt, maple syrup, and vanilla until thoroughly incorporated. Spread the yogurt mixture on the prepared baking sheet in a layer as thick as a chocolate bar.

Place small dollops of peanut butter and jam all over the yogurt. Using the tip of the fork, gently swirl the peanut butter and jam throughout the yogurt. Play around with the pattern and distribute them unevenly for variation.

Top with the frozen berries and peanuts, gently pressing them into the yogurt.

Freeze for at least 4 hours, or until completely solid. At this point, remove the parchment and break the yogurt into random bits by gently smashing it on the table. Put leftovers back in the freezer in a zip-top bag for up to 1 month!

INGREDIENTS

2 cups (480 g) full-fat plain Greek yogurt

1 tablespoon (20 g) maple syrup

1 teaspoon vanilla extract

2 tablespoons (32 g) smooth peanut butter

2 tablespoons (40 g) raspberry or strawberry jam

½ cup (75 g) mixed frozen berries

¼ cup (38 g) chopped peanuts

MY FAVORITE COOKIE: BANANA OATMEAL

YIELD: MAKES 8 TO 10 COOKIES

I love cookies but making them is always a hassle for me: You have to get the butter to that just-right room temperature, there are lots of ingredients and steps, and things can go wrong easily. This cookie, however, comes together in just one bowl and it's basically foolproof. It's also soooo much more nutritious. These cookies can be made ahead. Just store them in an airtight container for up to 5 days.

INSTRUCTIONS

Preheat the oven to 350°F (180°C, or gas mark 4). Line a baking sheet with parchment paper.

In a large bowl, using a fork, mash the bananas to a chunky consistency. Crack in the egg and add the vanilla. Whisk the egg into the bananas until thoroughly incorporated.

Sift in the flour and pour in the oats. Add the baking powder, cinnamon, and nutmeg. Use a spatula to mix everything until the dough is homogenous and all ingredients are incorporated.

Stir in the dark chocolate and walnuts (both optional, but highly recommended). I use chocolate chunks because I like their imperfect look, as opposed to chocolate chips.

Using a ¼-cup measure or ice cream scoop, scoop the dough onto the prepared baking sheet. You should get 8 to 10 cookies. Don't flatten the dough; it will naturally fall into a cookie shape while baking.

Bake for 12 to 15 minutes until slightly browned and still crumbly yet holding together. The cookies will be moist and crunchy. Sprinkle each with a touch of sea salt. Let cool for about 5 minutes and go to town.

INGREDIENTS

3 ripe or overripe bananas (preferably overripe)

1 large egg

Splash of vanilla extract

½ cup (60 g) all-purpose flour

1 cup (80 g) old-fashioned rolled oats

1 teaspoon baking powder

1 teaspoon ground cinnamon

½ teaspoon ground nutmeg

⅓ cup (57 g) dark chocolate chunks (70 percent cacao), plus more for topping (optional)

¼ cup (30 g) chopped walnuts (optional)

Flaky sea salt for topping

ACKNOWLEDGMENTS

This book couldn't have been possible without the hard work of many, many amazing humans.

I wanna thank my friend and creative director, Sonia, who helped day in, day out on the photo shoot. This book would not look the way it does if you were not a part of my team.

Thank you to all the wonderful people at Quarto: Thom, for believing in me and getting this book off the ground, as well as being insanely patient and motivating, providing guidance throughout this whole journey (I will miss our weekly chats); Mary, for the thoughtful collaboration while editing the recipes; John and Meredith, for the behind-the-scenes editorial help; and Regina, for making the book look exactly the way it should on the design front.

And although things might get a little cheesy now, I have to acknowledge my parents, who bought my first camera when I was 13 and supported me every step of the way in my journey as a creator, and my brother, who's just generally awesome.

Last but not least, Cristina, you have been right next to me through my best and worst moments. I will always love you for bringing beauty and joy into my life and making me the person I am today.

ABOUT THE AUTHOR

Kevin Tatar is a passionate home chef who loves finding fun ways to enjoy food and help others gain confidence in the kitchen. His mission is to unlock the world of home cooking for students (and young adults) everywhere. Kevin's cooking style and videos focus on four main things: affordability, nutrition, convenience, and enjoyment. He is proud to be a self-taught (nonprofessional) chef and wants his viewers to experience the cooking process vicariously through his videos. Find him as KWOOWK on TikTok, YouTube, and Instagram.

INDEX

A

Almond flakes, in Swiss Bircher Muesli, 44
Apple(s)
  Cinnamon Apple Crumble, 162
  Fresh Summer Quinoa Salad, 76
  Swiss Bircher Muesli, 44
Arborio rice, in Roasted Veggie Risotto, 117
Arugula
  The Best Black Bean Burger You'll Ever Eat,
    100–102
  Fresh Summer Quinoa Salad, 76
  My Triple-Decker Chicken Sandwich, 56–57
Avocado(s)
  Avocado Chocolate Mousse, 166
  Bacon, Avo, and Egg Breakfast Tacos, 51
  Custom Smoothie Bowls, 42–43
  Faster Than Fast Food Tacos, 96–97
  Fully Loaded Omelet, 48
  My Ultimate Chicken Taco Salad, 71–72
  Straightforward Black Bean Tacos, 143–145
  Superior Avocado Toast, 32

B

Bacon
  Bacon, Avo, and Egg Breakfast Tacos, 51
  Potato Breakfast Skillet for One, 38
Banana(s)
  Avocado Chocolate Mousse, 166
  Custom Smoothie Bowls, 42–43
  Healthy(ish) Banana Pancakes, 36
  My Favorite Cookie: Banana Oatmeal, 171
  Peanut Butter Banana Baked Oats, 35
  Personal Power Smoothie, 41
  Two-Ingredient Banana Soft Serve, 161
  Yogurt Parfait, 167
Basil (fresh)
  Herby Homemade Pesto Pasta with Tomatoes,
    120–121
  Spicy Cherry Tomato Pasta, 89
Beans. See also Black beans; Chickpeas
  canned, 14
  Faster Than Fast Food Tacos, 96–97
Beef. See Ground beef
Bell pepper(s)
  Chicken Fajita Pasta, 123
  The Leftover Fried Rice, 80–82
  Middle Eastern-Style Shakshuka, 47
  My Special Shakshuka, 52–53
  Roasted Veggie Risotto, 117
  Straightforward Black Bean Tacos, 143–145

The Ultimate Chicken and Broccoli Stir-Fry,
    103–105
Berries
  PB&J Frozen Yogurt Bark, 168
  Swiss Bircher Muesli, 44
  Yogurt Parfait, 167
Black beans
  The Best Black Bean Burger You'll Ever Eat,
    100–102
  Epic Tofu Burrito Bowl, 131–132
  Straightforward Black Bean Tacos, 143–145
Broccoli
  Loaded Veggie Quinoa Bowl, 135
  One-Pot Chicken and Broccoli Pasta,
    126–127
  The Ultimate Chicken and Broccoli Stir-Fry,
    103–105
Burgers
  The Best Black Bean Burger You'll Ever Eat,
    100–102
  Perfect Smash Burgers, 140–142
Burrito Bowl, Epic Tofu, 131–133
Burrito, folding a, 20
Butterflying, 18

C

Cabbage, in Tastiest Chicken Lunch Wrap, 63
Cake, Healthier Chocolate Lava, 158
Capers
  Leftover Chicken Salad, 86
  Mediterranean Pasta Salad, 75
  Tuna Melt Quesadilla, 64
Carrot(s)
  Custom Smoothie Bowls, 42–43
  My Creamy Veggie-Packed Soup, 90
  My Favorite Veggie Fritters, 155
  pickled, in Cheap Chicken Poke Bowl,
    128–130
Cauliflower Bites, Buffalo, 148–149
Cheddar cheese
  Fully Loaded Omelet, 48
  Healthy Buffalo Chicken Pita, 59
  Perfect Smash Burgers, 140–142
  Potato Breakfast Skillet for One, 38
  Spicy Cheesy Quesadillas, 146
  Tuna Melt Quesadilla, 64
Cheeses. See also Cheddar cheese; Feta
    cheese; Gouda cheese; Parmesan cheese
  gruyere, in Spicy Cheesy Quesadillas, 146
  pepper Jack, in Chicken Fajita Pasta, 123
  Romano, in Aglio e Olio e Cacio e Pepe,
    112–113
Cherry tomatoes
  Herby Homemade Pesto Pasta with Tomatoes,
    120–121
  Loaded Veggie Quinoa Bowl, 135
  Mediterranean Pasta Salad, 75

Roasted Veggie Risotto, 117
Spicy Cherry Tomato Pasta, 89
Chia seeds, in Custom Smoothie Bowls, 42–43
Chicken, 14
  Cheap Chicken Poke Bowl, 128–130
  Chicken Fajita Pasta, 123
  Creamy Dreamy Butter Chicken, 83–85
  Easy Chicken Congee, 95
  ground, in One-Pot Chicken and Broccoli Pas-
    ta, 126–127
  Healthier "Fried" Chicken Wings, 92–93
  Healthy Buffalo Chicken Pita, 59
  Leftover Chicken Salad, 86
  The Leftover Fried Rice, 80–82
  My Triple-Decker Chicken Sandwich, 56–57
  My Ultimate Chicken Taco Salad, 71–72
  Straightforward Chicken Breast, 25
  Tastiest Chicken Lunch Wrap, 63
  The Ultimate Chicken and Broccoli Stir-Fry,
    103–105
Chicken Tenders, Oven-Baked, 151
Chickpeas
  Chickpea Wrap, 60
  Creamy Chickpea Curry, 136
  Crispy Chickpea Sweet Potato Salad, 68–70
  My Special Shakshuka, 52–53
Chocolate
  Avocado Chocolate Mousse, 166
  Custom Smoothie Bowls, 42–43
  Healthier Chocolate Lava Cake, 158
  My Favorite Cookie: Banana Oatmeal, 171
Chopping ingredients, 19
Chorizo, in Fully Loaded Omelet, 48
Cilantro
  Bacon, Avo, and Egg Breakfast Tacos, 51
  Cheap Chicken Poke Bowl, 128–130
  Chickpea Wrap, 60
  Epic Tofu Burrito Bowl, 131–133
  Faster Than Fast Food Tacos, 96–97
  Fully Loaded Omelet, 48
  Healthy Buffalo Chicken Pita, 59
  Herby Yogurt Sauce and Dip, 26
  My Favorite Veggie Fritters, 155
  My Ultimate Chicken Taco Salad, 71–72
  Straightforward Black Bean Tacos, 143–145
  Tastiest Chicken Lunch Wrap, 63
Cocoa powder
  Custom Smoothie Bowls, 42–43
  Healthier Chocolate Lava Cake, 158
  Two-Ingredient Banana Soft Serve, 161
Coconut flakes, in Custom Smoothie Bowls,
    42–43
Coconut milk, in Creamy Chickpea Curry, 136
Cookie, Banana Oatmeal, 171
Corn
  Epic Tofu Burrito Bowl, 131–133
  My Ultimate Chicken Taco Salad, 71–72
  Straightforward Black Bean Tacos, 143–145

Cornflakes, in Oven-Baked Chicken Tenders, 151
Cranberries (dried)
    Fresh Summer Quinoa Salad, 76
    Leftover Chicken Salad, 86
    Peanut Butter Banana Baked Oats, 35
    Swiss Bircher Muesli, 44
    Yogurt Parfait, 167
Cucumber
    Cheap Chicken Poke Bowl, 128–130
    Fresh Summer Quinoa Salad, 76
    Mediterranean Pasta Salad, 75
Curry, Creamy Chickpea, 136

D
Deglazing a pan, 19
Dill (fresh)
    The Gourmet Egg Salad Bagel, 67
    My Triple-Decker Chicken Sandwich sauce, 57
    Superior Avocado Toast, 32

E
Egg(s), 14
    Bacon, Avo, and Egg Breakfast Tacos, 51
    Boiled Eggs, The Easy Way, 22
    Fully Loaded Omelet, 48
    The Gourmet Egg Salad Bagel, 67
    Instant Ramen Upgrade, 106
    The Leftover Fried Rice, 80–82
    Middle Eastern-Style Shakshuka, 47
    My Special Shakshuka, 52–53
    Peanut Butter Banana Baked Oats, 35
    Potato Breakfast Skillet for One, 38
    Superior Avocado Toast, 32
Eggplant
    My Special Shakshuka, 52–53
    Roasted Veggie Risotto, 117
Equipment, cooking and kitchen, 12–13

F
Fats, 14–15
Feta cheese
    The Best Black Bean Burger You'll Ever Eat, 100–102
    Mediterranean Pasta Salad, 75
    Middle Eastern-Style Shakshuka, 47
    My Special Shakshuka, 52–53
    Straightforward Black Bean Tacos, 143–145
Flour tortillas. See also Tortilla wraps
    Faster Than Fast Food Tacos, 96–97
    My Ultimate Chicken Taco Salad, 71–72
    Spicy Cheesy Quesadillas, 146
    Straightforward Black Bean Tacos, 143–145
Fond, 21

G
Ginger (fresh)
    Creamy Dreamy Butter Chicken, 83–85
    Easy Chicken Congee, 95
    Instant Ramen Upgrade, 106
    The Ultimate Chicken and Broccoli Stir-Fry, 103–105
Gouda cheese, 15
    Fully Loaded Omelet, 48
    Healthy Buffalo Chicken Pita, 59
    Potato Breakfast Skillet for One, 38
    Spicy Cheesy Quesadillas, 146
Greek yogurt, 17
    Herby Yogurt Sauce and Dip, 26
    Leftover Chicken Salad, 86
    PB&J Frozen Yogurt Bark, 168
    Swiss Bircher Muesli, 44
    Yogurt Parfait, 167
Ground beef
    Faster Than Fast Food Tacos, 96–97
    Perfect Smash Burgers, 140–142

H
Herbs, 17. See also specific herbs
Hot sauce
    Buffalo Cauliflower Bites, 148–149
    Epic Tofu Burrito Bowl, 131–133
    Faster Than Fast Food Tacos, 96–97
    Healthy Buffalo Chicken Pita, 59

I
Imitation crab, in Cheap Chicken Poke Bowl, 128–130
Ingredients, staple, 14–17
Instant Ramen Upgrade, 106

J
Jalapeño pepper(s)
    Potato Breakfast Skillet for One, 38
    Spicy Cheesy Quesadillas, 146
    Straightforward Black Bean Tacos, 143–145
Jam, in PB&J Frozen Yogurt Bark, 168

K
Kiwi, in Custom Smoothie Bowls, 42–43
Knives, 12–13

L
Lettuce(s)
    Faster Than Fast Food Tacos, 96–97
    Leftover Chicken Salad, 86
    My Ultimate Chicken Taco Salad, 71–72
    Perfect Smash Burgers, 140–142

M
Mint leaves
    Fresh Summer Quinoa Salad, 76
    Personal Power Smoothie, 41
Muesli, Swiss Bircher, 44
Mushrooms
    Creamy Mushroom Pasta, 124–125
    Fully Loaded Omelet, 48
    Instant Ramen Upgrade, 106

N
Nuts. See also Walnuts
    Avocado Chocolate Mousse, 166
    Herby Homemade Pesto Pasta with Tomatoes, 120–121
    PB&J Frozen Yogurt Bark, 168
    Personal Power Smoothie, 41
    Swiss Bircher Muesli, 44
    Two-Ingredient Banana Soft Serve, 161

O
Oats, 15
    Cinnamon Apple Crumble, 162
    Custom Smoothie Bowls, 42–43
    Healthier Chocolate Lava Cake, 158
    My Favorite Cookie: Banana Oatmeal, 171
    Peanut Butter Banana Baked Oats, 35
    Swiss Bircher Muesli, 44
Onions, pickled. See Pickled Red Onions (And Other Things)

P
Pancakes, Healthy(ish) Banana, 36
Parmesan cheese
    Creamy Mushroom Pasta, 124–125
    Herby Homemade Pesto Pasta with Tomatoes, 120–121
    Homemade Gnocchi with Peas and Walnuts, 108–110
    One-Pot Chicken and Broccoli Pasta, 126–127
    Oven-Baked Chicken Tenders, 151
    Parm-Crusted Potato Wedges, 152
    Roasted Veggie Risotto, 117
Parsley
    Aglio e Olio e Cacio e Pepe, 112–113
    Chickpea Wrap, 60
    Creamy Mushroom Pasta, 124–125
    Crispy Chickpea Sweet Potato Salad, 68–70
    The Gourmet Egg Salad Bagel, 67
    Herby Homemade Pesto Pasta with Tomatoes, 120–121
    Herby Yogurt Sauce and Dip, 26
    Homemade Gnocchi with Peas and Walnuts, 108–111
    Leftover Chicken Salad, 86

Loaded Veggie Quinoa Bowl, 135
Mediterranean Pasta Salad, 75
Middle Eastern-Style Shakshuka, 47
My Special Shakshuka, 52–53
One-Pot Chicken and Broccoli Pasta, 126–127
Tuna Melt Quesadilla, 64
Parsnips, in My Creamy Veggie-Packed Soup, 90
Pasta
  Aglio e Olio e Cacio e Pepe, 112–113
  Chicken Fajita Pasta, 123
  Creamy Mushroom Pasta, 124–125
  Herby Homemade Pesto Pasta with Tomatoes, 120–121
  Mediterranean Pasta Salad, 75
  My Mom's Walnut Dessert Pasta, 164–165
  One-Pot Chicken and Broccoli Pasta, 126–127
  salting water of, 21
  Spicy Cherry Tomato Pasta, 89
Peanut butter
  Custom Smoothie Bowls, 42–43
  PB&J Frozen Yogurt Bark, 168
  Peanut Butter Banana Baked Oats, 35
  Swiss Bircher Muesli, 44
Peanuts, in PB&J Frozen Yogurt Bark, 168
Peas (frozen)
  Cheap Chicken Poke Bowl, 128–130
  Homemade Gnocchi with Peas and Walnuts, 108–111
  Instant Ramen Upgrade, 106
  The Leftover Fried Rice, 80–82
  My Creamy Veggie-Packed Soup, 90
Pesto Pasta with Tomatoes, 120–121
Pickled carrots, in Cheap Chicken Poke Bowl, 128–130
Pickled Red Onions (And Other Things)
  The Best Black Bean Burger You'll Ever Eat, 100–102
  recipe, 24
  Straightforward Black Bean Tacos, 143–145
  Tastiest Chicken Lunch Wrap, 63
Pineapple, in Personal Power Smoothie, 41
Pita, Healthy Buffalo Chicken, 59
Potatoes
  Homemade Gnocchi with Peas and Walnuts, 108–111
  My Creamy Veggie-Packed Soup, 90
  Parm-Crusted Potato Wedges, 152
  Potato Breakfast Skillet for One, 38

Q
Quesadillas
  Spicy Cheesy Quesadillas, 146
  Tuna Melt Quesadilla, 64

Quinoa
  Fresh Summer Quinoa Salad, 76
  Loaded Veggie Quinoa Bowl, 135

R
Rice, 15, 17
  Cheap Chicken Poke Bowl, 128–130
  Creamy Chickpea Curry with, 136
  Easy Chicken Congee, 95
  Epic Tofu Burrito Bowl, 131–133
  The Leftover Fried Rice, 80–82
  Perfect Rice Every Time, 27
Rice noodles, in Sweet and Spicy Tofu Noodles, 114
Risotto, Roasted Veggie, 117
Rolled oats. See Oats

S
Salad dressings, formula for, 72
Sandwiches. See also Burgers
  The Gourmet Egg Salad Bagel, 67
  Leftover Chicken Salad, 86
  My Triple-Decker Chicken Sandwich, 56–57
Sautéing, 21
Shakshuka
  Middle Eastern-Style Shakshuka, 47
  My Special Shakshuka, 52–53
Smoothie Bowls, Custom, 42–43
Smoothie, Personal Power, 41
Soup, My Creamy Veggie-Packed, 90
Soy sauce, 17
Spices, 17
Spinach
  Custom Smoothie Bowls, 42–43
  Personal Power Smoothie, 41
Stir-frying, 21
Stir-Fry, The Ultimate Chicken and Broccoli, 103–105
Surimi (imitation crab), in Cheap Chicken Poke Bowl, 128–130
Sweeteners, 17
Sweet potatoes
  Crispy Chickpea Sweet Potato Salad, 68–70
  Loaded Veggie Quinoa Bowl, 135
  My Favorite Veggie Fritters, 155

T
Tacos
  Bacon, Avo, and Egg Breakfast Tacos, 51
  Faster Than Fast Food Tacos, 96–97
  Straightforward Black Bean Tacos, 143–145
Taco Salad, My Ultimate Chicken, 71–72
Tahini
  Crispy Chickpea Sweet Potato Salad dressing, 69

My Triple-Decker Chicken Sandwich sauce, 57
Superior Avocado Toast, 32
Techniques, 18–21
Tofu
  Epic Tofu Burrito Bowl, 131–133
  Sweet and Spicy Tofu Noodles, 114
Tomato(es). See also Cherry tomatoes
  The Best Black Bean Burger You'll Ever Eat, 100–102
  canned, in My Special Shakshuka, 52–53
  Epic Tofu Burrito Bowl, 131–133
  Faster Than Fast Food Tacos, 96–97
  Leftover Chicken Salad, 86
  My Triple-Decker Chicken Sandwich, 56–57
  My Ultimate Chicken Taco Salad, 71–72
  Perfect Smash Burgers, 140–142
  Superior Avocado Toast, 32
Tortillas, 17. See also Flour tortillas
  Chickpea Wrap, 60
  Tastiest Chicken Lunch Wrap, 63
  Tuna Melt Quesadilla, 64

V
Vegetables, 15
Veggie Stock
  My Creamy Veggie-Packed Soup, 90
  recipe, 23

W
Walnuts
  Cinnamon Apple Crumble, 162
  Custom Smoothie Bowls, 42–43
  Fresh Summer Quinoa Salad, 76
  Herby Homemade Pesto Pasta with Tomatoes, 120–121
  Homemade Gnocchi with Peas and Walnuts, 108–111
  Loaded Veggie Quinoa Bowl, 135
  My Favorite Cookie: Banana Oatmeal, 171
  My Mom's Walnut Dessert Pasta, 164–165
  Peanut Butter Banana Baked Oats, 35
Wraps
  Chickpea Wrap, 60
  Tastiest Chicken Lunch Wrap, 63

Y
Yogurt. See Greek yogurt

Z
Zucchini, in My Favorite Veggie Fritters, 155